JUMP BACK, PAUL

JUMP BACK, PAUL

THE LIFE AND POEMS OF PAUL LAURENCE DUNBAR

Sally Derby

ILLUSTRATED BY

Sean Qualls

CANDLEWICK PRESS

First edition 2015

Library of Congress Catalog Card Number 2014952480
ISBN 978-0-7636-6070-3

15 16 17 18 19 20 APS 10 9 8 7 6 5 4 3 2 1

Printed in Humen, Dongguan, China

This book was typeset in Esprit.
The illustrations were done in acrylic and pencil.

Candlewick Press
99 Dover Street
Somerville, Massachusetts 02144

visit us at www.candlewick.com

In tribute to Western College for Women,
site of Freedom Summer Volunteer Training, 1964.

The anchor still holds.
S. D.

For young, aspiring poets everywhere—
let your voices be heard!
S. Q.

1

You never heard of the poet Paul Laurence Dunbar? Child, where've you been? I got to have a word with you. Why, back in the day, you'd have whole families sitting around listening while one of them performed "When Malindy Sings" or "Little Brown Baby" or "A Negro Love Song" (which folks most always call "Jump Back, Honey").

And you notice I said "performed"? That's because Paul Dunbar's poems are meant for saying out loud, standing straight and proud. You don't just sit quiet with a book of them in your hand, reading the words to yourself. No, sir. You call out his poems in your very best voice, the way he did way back when.

Now, some of Paul's poems may give you a mite bit of trouble at first. Take "Jump Back, Honey." First time you see it printed you're likely gonna think, "What kind of poem's this? All those apostrophes. All those weird words, like *las'* in the very first line. And in line three, only the last two words look like real words to me."

But just relax and read the words the way they're spelled, it'll come to you quick. That line three you're complaining about? You read it exactly how the letters look and you'll hear, "Held her hand and squeezed it tight." Try it now, and you'll see what I mean.

A Negro Love Song

Seen my lady home las' night,
    Jump back, honey, jump back.
Hel' huh han' an' sque'z it tight,
    Jump back, honey, jump back.
Heahd huh sigh a little sigh,
Seen a light gleam f'um huh eye,
An' a smile go flittin' by —
    Jump back, honey, jump back.

Heahd de win' blow thoo de pines,
    Jump back, honey, jump back.
Mockin' bird was singin' fine,
    Jump back, honey, jump back.
An' my hea't was beatin' so,
When I reached my lady's do',
Dat I couldn't ba' to go —
    Jump back, honey, jump back.

Put my ahm aroun' huh wais',
    Jump back, honey, jump back.
Raised huh lips an' took a tase,
    Jump back, honey, jump back.
Love me, honey, love me true?
Love me well ez I love you?
An' she ansawhd: " 'Cose I do" —
    Jump back, honey, jump back.

That's a happy poem if there ever was one, don't you think? If all Paul's poems were like that, you'd probably think he was a happy man. And I don't want to get ahead of myself, but if I'm going to give you a true picture of Paul Dunbar, I have to show you another of his poems right here:

Disappointed

An old man planted and dug and tended,
    Toiling in joy from dew to dew:
The Sun was kind and the rain befriended:
    Fine grew his orchard and fair to view.
Then he said: "I will quiet my thrifty fears,
For here is fruit for my failing years."

But even then the storm-clouds gathered,
    Swallowing up the azure sky;
The sweeping winds into white foam lathered
    The placid breast of the bay, hard by;

3

Then the spirits that raged in the darkened air
Swept o'er his orchard and left it bare.

The old man stood in the rain, uncaring,
    Viewing the place the storm had swept;
And then with a cry from his soul despairing,
    He bowed him down to the earth, and wept.
But a voice cried aloud from the driving rain:
"Arise, old man, and plant again!"

Almost like two different men wrote those two poems, isn't it? Keep that in mind while we're going along with the story, because it'll come up again.

I'm thinking now about where to start. I suppose the first thing you ought to know is that Paul's mama and daddy, Matilda and Joshua Dunbar, were born slaves. But by the time Paul was born, in 1872, that long, hard Civil War had been over for seven years, so Paul was born free, right here in Dayton, Ohio. Still, you hear some of his poems, you'll find out he wasn't a stranger to slavery days. That's because all his life long he listened to people's rememberings.

His mama, now, she liked telling about life in the slave cabins—everyday goings-on, especially the funny ones. Even when Paul was grown, he liked to listen to old folks talking about their lives, and sometimes he'd turn their memories into poems.

Opportunity

Granny's gone a-visitin',
     Seen huh git huh shawl
W'en I was a-hidin' down
     Hime de gyahden wall.
Seen huh put her bonnet on,
     Seen huh tie de strings,
An' I'se gone to dreamin' now
     'Bout dem cakes an' t'ings.

On de she'f behime de do'—
     Mussy, what a feas'!
Soon ez she gits out o' sight,
     I kin eat in peace.
I bin watchin' fu' a week
     Des fu' dis hyeah chance.
Mussy, w'en I gits in daih,
     I'll des sholy dance.

Lemon pie an' gingah-cake,
     Let me set an' t'ink—
Vinegah an' sugah, too,
     Dat 'll mek a drink;
Ef dey's one t'ing dat I loves
     Mos' pu'ticlahly,
It is eatin' sweet t'ings an'
     A-drinkin' Sangaree.

Lawdy, won' po' granny raih
     W'en she see de she'f;

W'en I t'ink erbout huh face,
   I's mos' 'shamed myse'f.
Well, she gone, an' hyeah I is,
   Back behime de do'—
Look hyeah! Gran' 's done 'spected me,
   Dain't no sweets no mo'.

Evah sweet is hid erway,
   Job des done up brown;
Pusson t'ink dat someun t'ought
   Dey was t'eves erroun';
Dat des breaks my heart in two,
   Oh how bad I feel!
Des to t'ink my own gramma
   B'lieved dat I 'u'd steal!

Now, Paul's daddy, Joshua, he was a bitter man. Growing up a slave, he swallowed such a heap of anger, he knew he had to either escape or explode. Exploding would be easier, but it would likely get him "sold down the river." That was the slave's way of saying your master decided you were too hardheaded for Kentucky, so he sold you to a slave owner down South—like in Alabama or Louisiana. You didn't want that to happen, no, sir. So Joshua bided his time and made himself useful by learning to plaster. He got so good at plastering he was sometimes hired out to other plantations. That way, he saw more of the country round about.

He studied his chances, and when the right opportunity came, he ran away to Canada, escaping by way of the Underground Railroad. (I expect you've heard of that, right?)

While he was living up there, back in this country, the Civil War began, and after a while, he heard that President Lincoln had freed all the slaves, and that the Union army was enlisting colored soldiers. ("Colored"—that's what they called blacks then, honey, or "Negro" if they wanted to be specially polite.) Right away, Joshua came back across the border to join up.

More than one of Paul's poems was inspired by his dad's Civil War stories, but I've always wondered if Joshua talked about what it was like being in the U.S. Colored Troops. Did he explain how he enlisted in a *Massachusetts* infantry regiment because it was one of the first that was ready and willing to accept Negro volunteers? Then, after all the marching and standing around made the veins in his legs swell so bad that the regiment gave him a medical discharge—did he say how he felt about that? I reckon it didn't make him feel happy, because he reenlisted, this time in the Fifth Massachusetts Colored Cavalry (where the legs of his horse could do all the work). Did he ever mention wounds or deaths, any of soldiering's miseries? Or was it all prideful talk about courage and battles and medals that Paul heard from Joshua?

from When Dey 'Listed Colored Soldiers

Dey was talkin' in de cabin, dey was talkin' in de
    hall;
But I listened kin' o' keerless, not a-t'inkin' 'bout it all;
An' on Sunday, too, I noticed, dey was whisp'rin'
    mighty much,

Stan'in' al erroun' de roadside w'en dey let us out
     o' chu'ch.
But I did n't t'ink erbout it 'twell de middle of de week,
An' my 'Lias come to see me, an' somehow he could n't
     speak.
Den I seed all in a minute whut he 'd come to see me
     for;—
Dey had 'listed colo'ed sojers, an' my 'Lias gwine
     to wah.

Oh, I hugged him, an' I kissed him, an' I baiged him not
     to go;
But he tol' me dat his conscience, hit was callin' to him
     so,
An' he could n't baih to lingah w'en he had a chanst to
     fight
For de freedom dey had gin him an' de glory of de right.
So he kissed me, an' he lef' me, w'en I 'd p'omised to be
     true;
An' dey put a knapsack on him, an' a coat all colo'ed
     blue.
So I gin him pap's ol' Bible f'om de bottom of de
     draw',—
W'en dey 'listed colo'ed sojers an' my 'Lias went to
     wah.

Sometime after the war was over, Paul's mama and daddy met. Matilda Burton Murphy was a pretty young widow with two small sons. William Travis, who was always called Buddy, was seven, and Robert Small, called

9

Rob, was five. Joshua declared himself ready to marry and settle down. But it takes a lot of patience to step-dad two small boys, and patience wasn't Joshua's strong suit. All the anger he'd grown up with was still there, right below the surface, ready to erupt at the least little thing. When that happened, Matilda and her boys had better watch out.

Things didn't get better when Paul was born. Matter of fact, they went downhill fast. Joshua was almost fifty by now, and plastering jobs were hard to come by, not to mention hard on the legs and back. Life wasn't doing anything to sweeten Joshua's disposition. Then, a few months before Paul turned two, Matilda birthed a baby girl.

Elizabeth Florence, or Liza, as they called her, was a sickly baby, and Joshua never warmed up to her. Seems like he'd had his fill of parenthood. He began to spend more and more time away from home. Matilda had to look to her sons for help. Buddy and Rob could run errands and do odd jobs around the neighborhood to bring in a few pennies. Paul's job was to rock and amuse Liza as much as he could. Liza wasn't even a year old when Joshua moved out. I reckon everyone breathed a mite easier with his anger and beatings gone.

It wasn't like Joshua was heartless. I'm not excusing the beatings, but life had treated Joshua rough. Raised a slave, how could he know what family life could be like? After he left, Joshua sometimes sent Matilda money for this or that. Once in a while, he would even come back for a spell, so he and Matilda could try again.

Then maybe, for a while, Joshua might have been the kind of father Paul would write about later:

Little Brown Baby

Little brown baby wif spa'klin' eyes,
    Come to yo' pappy an' set on his knee.
What you been doin', suh—makin' san' pies?
    Look at dat bib—you 's ez du'ty ez me.
Look at dat mouf—dat 's merlasses, I bet;
    Come hyeah, Maria, an' wipe off his han's.
Bees gwine to ketch you an' eat you up yit,
    Bein' so sticky an sweet—goodness lan's!

Little brown baby wif spa'klin' eyes,
    Who 's pappy's darlin' an' who 's pappy's chile?
Who is it all de day nevah once tries
    Fu' to be cross, er once loses dat smile?
Whah did you git dem teef? My, you 's a scamp!
    Whah did dat dimple come f'om in yo' chin?
Pappy do' know yo—I b'lieves you 's a tramp;
    Mammy, dis hyeah 's some ol' straggler got in!

Let 's th'ow him outen de do' in de san',
    We do' want stragglers a-layin' 'roun' hyeah;
Let 's gin him 'way to de big buggah-man;
    I know he 's hidin' erroun' hyeah right neah.
Buggah-man, buggah-man, come in de do',
    Hyeah's a bad boy you kin have fu' to eat.
Mammy an' pappy do' want him no mo',
    Swaller him down f'om his haid to his feet!

Dah, now, I t'ought dat you 'd hug me up close.
    Go back, ol' buggah, you sha'n't have dis boy.

He ain't no tramp, ner no straggler, of co'se;
　He 's pappy's pa'dner an' playmate an' joy.
Come to you' pallet now—go to yo' res';
　Wisht you could allus know ease an' cleah skies;
Wisht you could stay jes' a chile on my breas'—
　Little brown baby wif spa'klin' eyes!

But Joshua's good resolves never lasted, and an on-again, off-again husband isn't what you'd call a good provider. In January of 1876, Matilda filed for divorce. Four months later, a month before Paul's fourth birthday, his little sister died.

So there was Matilda, a black woman who'd never been taught to read or write, with no man offering steady support for the family. How was she going to raise three little boys all by herself?

By hard work, that's how. She took in laundry from Dayton's downtown hotels to earn the money for food and rent. She washed and starched and hung out clothes. She ironed sheets and pillowcases. And she did it all by hand. Dayton didn't have electricity then, so it was washboards and clotheslines and flatirons. (You try that someday, child, and you'll know what hard work is.)

After she'd worked her way through the day's wash, Matilda had to set about fixing supper. Any mama will tell you that a growing boy is just one big appetite, and Paul and his brothers weren't any different. Sometimes when it seemed to the boys the meal would never be ready, Matilda would tell them a story or two to ease the waiting. Matilda's stories were always funny, even when they were about things that happened when she was growing up a slave in

Kentucky. Food for his body and stories for his soul — what more could Paul want?

from **When de Co'n Pone's Hot**

When you set down at de table,
    Kin' o' weary lak an' sad,
An' you'se jes' a little tiahed
    An' purhaps a little mad;
How yo' gloom tu'ns into gladness,
    How yo' joy drives out de doubt
When de oven do' is opened,
    An' de smell comes po'in' out;
Why, de 'lectric light o' Heaven
    Seems to settle on de spot,
When yo' mammy ses de blessin'
    An' de co'n pone's hot.

When de cabbage pot is steamin'
    An' de bacon good an' fat,
When de chittlins is a sputter'n'
    So's to show you whah dey's at;
Take away yo' sody biscuit,
    Take away yo' cake an' pie,
Fu' de glory time is comin',
    An' it's 'proachin' very nigh,
An' you want to jump an' hollah,
    Do you know you'd bettah not,
When yo' mammy ses de blessin'
    An' de co'n pone's hot.

If you're wondering what it was like growing up back then, you read Paul's stories and poems, you'll get a good idea. To me, it stands to reason that Paul and his friends must have been as full of energy and devilment as you and your friends are. (There's two story poems, "The Rivals" and "The Spellin' Bee," that would show you real well. We'd be sitting a long, long time if I tried to tell you all Paul's poems, but maybe you'll want to find those two and read them by yourself.)

In those days, boys and girls had most of their fun outside, because what was there to do indoors? And Dayton's a good place for playing outdoors — hot, lazy summers with rivers close by; cold, snowy winters with plenty of hills for sledding. You'd finish your chores as early as you could, then out you went to freedom and fun.

from A Grievance

W'en de snow 's a-fallin'
    An' de win' is col'.
Mammy 'mence a-callin',
    Den she 'mence to scol',
"Lucius Lishy Brackett,
    Don't you go out do's,
Button up yo' jacket,
    Les'n you 'll git froze."

I sit at de windah
    Lookin' at de groun',

Nuffin nigh to hindah,
    Mammy ain' erroun';
. . . .
Bet in a half a minute
    I fly out de do'
An' I 's knee-deep in it,
    Dat dah blessed snow.

Den I hyeah a pattah
    Come acrost de flo'.
Den dey comes a clattah
    At de cabin do';
An' my mammy holler
    Spoilin' all my joy,
"Come in f'om dat waller,
    Don't I see you, boy?"

W'en de snow 's a-sievin'
    Down ez sof' ez meal,
Whut 's de use o' livin'
    'Cept you got de feel
Of de stuff dat 's fallin'
    'Roun' an' white an' damp,
'Dout some one a-callin',
    "Come in hyeah, you scamp!"

2

Matilda Dunbar loved her older boys, Rob and Buddy, but it was Paul she had high hopes for. From the first, she was certain he would amount to something, give him half a chance. And she was going to make sure he got all the chances he needed. One of the first things she did was teach herself to read and write. Paul might grow up poor, but he would have a mother he was proud of. (To my way of thinking, someone should write Matilda's own story someday. Seems like there was nothing she couldn't do once she set her mind to it.)

Like many young boys and girls then, Buddy and Rob quit school and went to work when they were barely in their teens. Matilda wasn't going to let that happen to Paul. In her heart of hearts, she was hoping Paul would grow up to become a preacher. No reason he couldn't—he was smart, he was well spoken (she took pride in his correct diction and wide vocabulary), and he had learned from his daddy how to carry himself like a soldier, all dignified and proud. When he was old enough, she might let him work before or after school, on weekends maybe, or during the summer, but for sure he was going to stay in school.

In those days it was some easier than now for boys to find paying jobs. Depending on the time of year, you could sell papers, mow grass, rake leaves, shovel snow, do all kinds of odd jobs. And one year Paul got himself a job that just about any boy would like.

Every day as evening came on, crews of boys would go out, each one carrying his own ladder and holding a torch. The boys would head out in different directions, trudging up and down streets, going from street lamp to street lamp, all over town. They'd prop their ladder against the lamppost, climb up, and turn on the gas. Soon as the gas came hissing out, they'd hold their torch to it, and the gas would burst into flame, chasing away the darkness. Lamplighters, that's what the boys were called.

But Paul's first year at the job turned out to be his last. That summer, workers started setting tall poles and stringing wires, street after street. When they were done, electricity came to Dayton. Wonderful as it was, you couldn't blame Paul if he sighed just a bit — there went his job, and all the new wires made it a sight harder to find a good place to fly a kite.

At Candle-Lightin' Time

When I come in f'om de co'n-fiel' aftah wo'kin' ha'd
      all day,
It 's amazin' nice to fin' my suppah all erpon de way;
An' it 's nice to smell de coffee bubblin' ovah in
      de pot,
An' it 's fine to see de meat a-sizzlin' teasin'-lak
      an' hot.

But when suppah-time is ovah, an' de t'ings is
      cleahed away;
Den de happy hours dat foller are de sweetes' of
      de day.
When my co'ncob pipe is sta'ted, an' de smoke is
      drawin' prime,
My ole 'ooman says, "I reckon, Ike, it's candle-lightin'
      time."

Den de chillun snuggle up to me, an' all commence
      to call,
"Oh, say, daddy, now it's time to mek de shadders
      on de wall."
So I puts my han's togethah—evah daddy knows
      de way,—
An' de chillun snuggle closer roun' ez I begin to
      say:—
"Fus' thing, hyeah come Mistah Rabbit; don' you see
      him wo'k his eahs?"

19

Huh, uh! dis mus' be a donkey,—look, how innercent
    he 'pears!
Dah 's de ole black swan a-swimmin'—ain't she
    got a' awful neck?
Who 's dis feller dat 's a-comin'? Why, dat's ole dog
    Tray, I 'spec'!"

Dat 's de way I run on, tryin' fu' to please 'em all I can;
Den I hollahs, "Now be keerful—dis hyeah las' 's de
    buga-man!"
An' dey runs an' hides dey faces; dey ain't skeered—
    dey's lettin' on:
But de play ain't raaly ovah twell dat buga-man is
    gone.

So I jes' teks up my banjo, an' I plays a little chune,
An' you see dem haids come peepin' out to listen
    mighty soon.
Den my wife says, "Sich a pappy fu' to give you sich
    a fright!
Jes' you go to baid, an' leave him: say yo' prayers an'
    say good-night."

Now, school—I want to tell you about that. Housing problems kept Matilda and the boys on the move. Paul went to three different schools, called district schools, before he even got to the eighth grade. But somehow he still did real well. The only subject he didn't get good grades in was mathematics. Seemed like he couldn't keep his mind on numbers; it was words he loved from the start. When he wasn't reading, he was writing. From the time he was little, he loved playing around with rhyming words.

Dayton wasn't so big then, of course, and Ohio law didn't say you had to stay in school till you were eighteen, like it does now. All the eighth-graders in the whole city could fit in just one school, called the Intermediate School. Those days, many families thought eight years of school was plenty, so each class starting in at Central High School, the only high school the city had then, was considerably smaller than it'd been at Intermediate.

Paul had just turned thirteen and was about to enter eighth grade when Joshua Dunbar died, so now there was no more support from him. About the same time, Buddy and Rob, who had been bringing home the money they earned, went off to start their own families. So now it was just Matilda and Paul. Paul was strong and healthy for the most part, although he had what folks called a weak chest. (I'll tell you more about that later.) Probably about then, some folks started hinting around to Matilda that it was time for Paul to find work and support her, but if they did, she didn't listen. Matilda had her own ideas. This youngest son of hers loved learning and got good grades. When the time came, he was going to high school. They would get by somehow. She would see to it.

You wondering how Paul felt about this? By all accounts, that was fine with him. He always said his school years were good years. He had teachers who encouraged him, he had lots of good friends, and he liked book learning. But whenever I read "In the Morning," I catch myself thinking that once in a while, at getting-up time, even a boy who likes school a lot might want to stay in bed a little bit longer.

from "In the Morning"

'Lias! 'Lias! Bless de Lawd!
Don' you know de day's erbroad?
Ef you don' git up, you scamp,
Dey 'll be trouble in dis camp.
T'ink I gwine to let you sleep
W'ile I meks yo' boa'd an' keep?
Dat 's a putty howdy-do—
Don' you hyeah me, 'Lias—you?

. . . .

'Lias, don' you hyeah me call?
No use tu'ning to'ds de wall;
I kin hyeah dat mattuss squeak;
Don' you hyeah me w'en I speak?
Dis hyeah clock done struck off six—
Ca'line, bring me dem ah sticks!
Oh, you down, suh; huh! you down—
Look hyeah, don' you daih to frown.

Ma'ch yo'se'f an' wash yo' face,
Don' you splattah all de place;
I got somep'n else to do,
'Sides jes' cleanin' aftah you.
Tek dat comb an' fix yo' haid—
Looks jes' lak a feddah baid.
Look hyeah, boy, I let you see
You sha' n't roll yo' eyes at me.

. . . .

Fol' yo' han's an' bow yo' haid—
Wait ontwell de blessin' 's said;

"Lawd, have mussy on ouah souls—"
(Don' you daih to tech dem rolls—)
"Bless de food we gwine to eat—"
(You set still—I see yo' feet;
You jes' try dat trick agin!)
"Gin us peace an' joy. Amen!"

Central High School was the only high school in Dayton, and Paul was the only black student in his class. But he didn't let that worry him for a minute—he had himself a fine old time there. He got along with just about everyone—boys, girls, black, white, made no difference to him. It wasn't too long until his friends gave him a nickname. And didn't Matilda swell with pride when she learned they called him Deacon Dunbar! For sure, she thought, he was on his way to becoming a preacher.

One friend of Paul's was someone he'd known since grade school: William Burns, who everyone called Bud. Bud Burns was a year younger than Paul, and he was studying to become a doctor. (Mighty big dream for a colored boy in those days, but Bud made it; he became the first black member of the Dayton Medical Academy.) He and Paul stayed friends all their lives. In fact, whenever Paul was in Dayton, Bud did his doctoring.

In high school, Paul made a new friend named Orville Wright. Now, don't tell me you haven't heard that name before. You can't grow up in this country without learning about how Orville and Wilbur, the Wright brothers, built their own airplane and made one of the first real airplane flights at Kitty Hawk, North Carolina. That was later, of course. Now the brothers spent all their spare time in their bicycle shop. They had a printing press there, too. *West Side News* was the name of the newspaper they printed and sold. Paul wrote some articles for it, and then he decided to try to publish a newspaper especially for the black community.

Orville and Wilbur helped Paul get started. He called his paper the *Dayton Tattler*. But times were hard — times are most always hard, it seems — and Paul's neighbors didn't have any leftover nickels to spend on a newspaper, so he put out only a few issues before he had to give up on it.

But that didn't mean he was out of ideas. Writing just came natural to Paul, particularly writing poems. Matilda saved each one carefully, and she already had a boxful of them. Paul's poetry showed how much he had learned from reading the famous poems in his schoolbooks. Like those poems, his own poems were formal in form, subject, and language, and I doubt anyone who read them would guess they were written by a boy still in his teens. The teachers at Central were always praising them and encouraging Paul to write more. His friends said his poems were just as good as any they'd read in school. So he began to dream. In those days, lots of newspapers published poems. Wouldn't it be a fine thing to see one of his poems in Dayton's newspaper, the *Herald*?

Getting a poem published, now — that's easier dreamed of than done. Paul sent out poem after poem to the local newspaper, and poem after poem was sent back. But finally the *Herald* published one of his poems, "Our Martyred Soldiers," and then another, "On the River." Only sixteen years old and already a published writer! Jump back!

On the River

The sun is low,
The waters flow,
My boat is dancing to and fro.
The eve is still,
Yet from the hill
The killdeer echoes loud and shrill.

The paddles plash,
The wavelets dash,
We see the summer lightning flash;
While now and then,
In marsh and fen
Too muddy for the feet of men,

Where neither bird
Nor beast has stirred,
The spotted bullfrog's croak is heard.
The wind is high,
The grasses sigh,
The sluggish stream goes sobbing by.

And far away
The dying day
Has cast its last effulgent ray;
While on the land
The shadows stand
Proclaiming that the eve's at hand.

Well, graduation time came round, and Paul's class asked him to write words for the song they would sing at the ceremony. Those boys and girls had been going to school most of their lives, but now they had to go out and start finding their own way. Don't you think they were a mite scared? And maybe a little sad? Paul had the same feelings as the rest of them. How was he going to put all that in a song? He decided to compare himself and his friends to little boats just beginning their first voyage. I'm not going to tell you the whole of it, but I always liked these lines special because they show how everybody was feeling about leaving Central High and looking to their future:

> And now, the world we fear no more,
> As here we stand upon the shore,
> Prepared to cast our moorings free,
> And breast the waves of future's sea.
>
> . . . .
>
> At last we move, how thrills the heart,
> So long impatient for the start!
> Now up o'er hill and down through dell,
> The echoes bring our song — farewell.

I don't suppose anyone in the audience that day was any prouder than Matilda Dunbar was. Sure, it was Paul who was receiving a diploma, it was Paul who wrote the song his classmates were singing, but it was Matilda, born a slave forbidden to learn to read or write, who had made it possible.

3

SYMPATHY · COLORED · KNOWN · REACHED · BROTHERS

When Paul commenced job hunting that June, his head and his hopes were high. Wasn't he a high-school graduate? Didn't folks say he was a well-spoken young man? He'd heard girls call him intelligent, handsome. He didn't let all that go to his head, though. (If he'd started acting a little cocky, Matilda would have brought him down for sure.) He didn't see any reason he shouldn't feel good about himself and hopeful about his future.

But there was a reason, all right, and he realized it mighty quick. He was a Negro, and the first Civil Rights Act was a long time ahead. At Central, the fact that Paul was colored hadn't mattered much, but Paul knew that outside of school it mattered a lot. Fact is, bad feeling toward black people had been growing all the years Paul was in school. Some places black folks could live, and some places they couldn't. Some jobs black folks could have, and some jobs only whites could get.

Still, the *Herald* had published two of Paul's poems, hadn't they? They already knew he was a good writer. And now he had more than his poems to show — he had a high-school diploma! So dressed in his best, poems and diploma in hand, Paul marched himself down to the *Herald* offices to apply for a job as a reporter. In spite of all he knew about the world outside school, he must have felt like a bucket of cold water was being emptied on him when the response was a flat-out no. The only Negroes at newspaper offices, the editor told him, were the ones hired to sweep floors and empty spittoons. Coloreds didn't sit at a desk in the editorial room, no matter how well they could write.

Not even thirty years had gone by since the Emancipation Proclamation had freed America's slaves. Now here was Paul in Dayton, Ohio, the city that had been the last spot on the Underground Railroad for many of the passengers on their way to freedom. And here were people who acted like they didn't know that blacks as well as whites had fought for the Union during the Civil War.

Later on, when Paul wrote "The Colored Soldiers," one of his angriest poems, maybe he wasn't just remembering his dad's soldiering. Maybe the anger in it came from memories of this early rejection and humiliation.

from The Colored Soldiers

Yes, the Blacks enjoy their freedom
    And they won it dearly, too;
For the life blood of their thousands
    Did the southern fields bedew.

In the darkness of their bondage,
    In the depths of slavery's night;
Their muskets flashed the dawning
    And they fought their way to light.

They were comrades then and brothers,
    Are they more or less to-day?
They were good to stop a bullet
    And to front the fearful fray.
They were citizens and soldiers,
    When rebellion raised its head;
And the traits that made them worthy—
    Ah! those virtues are not dead.

They have shared your nightly vigils,
    They have shared your daily toil;
And their blood with yours commingling
    Has made rich the Southern soil.
They have slept and marched and suffered
    'Neath the same dark skies as you,
They have met as fierce a foeman
    And have been as brave and true.

And their deeds shall find a record,
    In the registry of Fame;
For their blood has cleansed completely
    Every blot of Slavery's shame.
So all honor and all glory
    To those noble Sons of Ham—
The gallant colored soldiers,
    Who fought for Uncle Sam!

Door after door closed in Paul's face. At the end of the summer, he took what he could get: a job running the elevator in downtown Dayton's Callahan Building.

Now, that elevator he drove — I wonder 'bout that. I was never in the Callahan Building, but some of those old-timey elevators closed you in with two doors, not just one. The inside one, it wasn't solid, but folded and opened up kinda like the gate you put at the top of the steps to keep the baby from tumbling down or in a doorway so the dog doesn't try to take a nap on the sofa. Every time that inside door was closed, it was just like being shut in a cage. I've wondered a lot if the memory of that elevator mightn't have inspired the metaphor Paul used in this famous poem:

Sympathy

I know what the caged bird feels, alas!
    When the sun is bright on the upland slopes;
When the wind stirs soft through the springing grass,
And the river flows like a stream of glass;
    When the first bird sings and the first bud opes,
And the faint perfume from its chalice steals —
I know what the caged bird feels!

I know why the caged bird beats his wing
    Till its blood is red on the cruel bars;
For he must fly back to his perch and cling
When he fain would be on the bough a-swing;
    And a pain still throbs in the old, old scars

And they pulse again with a keener sting—
I know why he beats his wing!

I know why the caged bird sings, ah me,
    When his wing is bruised and his bosom sore,—
When he beats his bars and he would be free;
It is not a carol of joy or glee,
    But a prayer that he sends from his heart's deep
        core,
But a plea, that upward to Heaven he flings—
I know why the caged bird sings!

Up and down. Up and down. Paul wasn't going anywhere. Must have been downright discouraging for a young
man who'd had such big dreams. But if his body couldn't
travel far, his mind could. And when no one was needing a
trip up or down, Paul pulled out his notebook and wrote. At
home that stack of poems his mother was keeping in a box in
the kitchen grew and grew.

When Lady Luck finally decided to smile, Paul was ready.
One day, the passenger who stepped into his elevator just
happened to be one of his old teachers, a Mrs. Helen M.
Truesdell. She asked if he was still writing, and when he
allowed he was, she told him a big convention of poets, the
Western Association of Writers, would be meeting in Dayton
that June. Would he like to read some of his poems to them?
    Would he? Jump back, honey! On June 27, 1892, Paul's
twentieth birthday, he took time off work to walk over to

Dayton's Grand Opera House. When he was called to the stage, he read a poem, the kind called an occasional poem, that he'd written especially for that day, that group. The minute he finished reading the last lines, the clapping began:

A welcome warm as Western wine,
And free as Western hearts, be thine.
Do what the greatest joy insures, —
The city has no will but yours!

Folks were mighty impressed, but Paul couldn't stick around for compliments and suchlike. He had to scoot back to work.

Lucky for Paul, James Newton Matthews heard about this talented young poet. Matthews was a doctor and a poet, not a newspaperman, but he had a newspaperman's nose for a good story, so he began sniffing around. He found out where Paul worked and took himself over to the Callahan Building. It didn't bother him that Paul couldn't take a few minutes off from the job — he just rode up and down like he was stuck to the side of the elevator and asked Paul all kinds of questions about his life and work.

A month or so later, back in Illinois, Dr. Matthews wrote a letter to his local paper. The letter quoted some of Paul's poems, and then it talked about how sad it was that such a talented young man was "chained like a galley slave to the ropes of a dingy elevator at starvation wages." Sure, that was an exaggeration, but it was the kind of thing folks

like to read, and it was reprinted in newspapers all over the country.

Just like that, Paul began getting "fan mail" from as far away as Rhode Island and Canada. To his mind, the best letter (maybe not counting the one from Canada that included twenty dollars to buy books) was from another poet, James Whitcomb Riley of Indiana. The Hoosier Poet — that's what they called Riley, and his poems were printed regular in newspapers all over the country. In his letter to Paul, Riley called him "my chirping young friend" and said Paul was "a singer who should command wide and serious attention."

Paul had got compliments on his writing before — from friends, from teachers, from folks at church — but this felt different. This praise was from a real poet. James Whitcomb Riley had more published books than Paul could name, and here he was predicting that Paul and his poems would become famous! Jump back!

I'm guessing that now Paul began to prick up his ears anytime he heard people talk about Riley. Why was Riley so famous, and why did so many people know and love his poems? Well, for one thing, Riley traveled around a lot. All over Ohio and Indiana. When Riley came to town, people paid good money and packed auditoriums just to hear him perform his poems. That's right: perform. Just like "A Negro Love Song," Riley's poems want to be heard — they about beg for you to open your mouth and let the words sing out. Take "Little Orphant Annie." The best way to hear that one is curled up in a big old armchair next to someone you love, and the best time to listen to it is in the evening just before the lights get turned on. You want it kind of shivery when you hear that poem.

Little Orphant Annie

James Whitcomb Riley

Little Orphant Annie's come to our house to stay,
An' wash the cups an' saucers up, an' brush the
      crumbs away,
An' shoo the chickens off the porch, an' dust the
      hearth, an' sweep,
An' make the fire, an' bake the bread, an' earn her
      board-an'-keep;
An' all us other childern, when the supper-things is
      done,
We set around the kitchen fire an' has the mostest fun
A-list'nin' to the witch-tales 'at Annie tells about,
An' the Gobble-uns 'at gits you
Ef you
Don't
Watch
Out!

Wunst they wuz a little boy wouldn't say his
      prayers,—
An' when he went to bed at night, away up-stairs,
His Mammy heerd him holler, an' his Daddy heerd
      him bawl,
An' when they turn't the kivvers down, he wuzn't
      there at all!
An' they seeked him in the rafter-room, an' cubby-
      hole, an' press,
An' seeked him up the chimbly-flue, an' ever'-wheres,
      I guess;

But all they ever found wuz thist his pants an'
  roundabout: —
An' the Gobble-uns 'll git you
Ef you
Don't
Watch
Out!

An' one time a little girl 'ud allus laugh an' grin,
An' make fun of ever' one, an' all her blood-an'-kin;
An' wunst, when they was "company," an' ole folks
  wuz there,
She mocked 'em an' shocked 'em, an' said she didn't
  care!
An' thist as she kicked her heels, an' turn't to run an'
  hide,
They wuz two great big Black Things a-standin' by
  her side,
An' they snatched her through the ceilin' 'fore she
  knowed what she's about!
An' the Gobble-uns 'll git you
Ef you
Don't
Watch
Out!

An' little Orphant Annie says, when the blaze is blue,
An' the lamp-wick sputters, an' the wind goes
  woo-oo!
An' you hear the crickets quit, an' the moon is gray,

An' the lightnin'-bugs in dew is all squenched
     away,—
You better mind yer parunts, an' yer teachurs fond an'
     dear,
An' churish them 'at loves you, an' dry the orphant's
     tear,
An' he'p the pore an' needy ones 'at clusters all
     about,
Er the Gobble-uns 'll git you
Ef you
Don't
Watch
Out!

Did you ever hear anyone whose way of talking was kind of like that poem? I'm guessing not. Seems to me, first thing you know, we're all going to talk like the reporters and the pretty people they call anchors on TV—everybody all the same.

Well, no matter. Riley wrote "Little Orphant Annie" and a sight of other poems in what they call Hoosier dialect—what he heard growing up in Indiana.

You remember I was telling you how Paul's poems were influenced by the poetry he was introduced to in school? He knew and loved poems by many of the greats—Keats, Shelley, Wordsworth—but here was someone who wrote poems in dialect, everyday speech about everyday things. (Some of them even used humor, and Paul loved a good joke.) Paul had already written a few poems in dialect, more for his own enjoyment than for anything else. Reading James Whitcomb Riley's poetry might have given him a glimpse of something that could be. The Hoosier dialect Riley used gave his Indiana poems color and richness — a feeling of being true to life. The dialect of southern Ohio blacks was every bit as rich, Paul felt. He could use the words, the turns of phrase, and the speech patterns of his friends and neighbors to bring the same richness to his own poems. And maybe people would want to read his dialect poems just as they wanted to read Riley's.

It's not like I was there, and I can't go to Paul and ask him, but in my heart of hearts, I believe what I've just told you is likely just the way it was.

4

ANTE-BELLUM SERMON A POET AND HIS SONGS

UNSLING HEROES

I don't suppose it was only on account of Riley's letter, but what with one thing and another, right about then, Paul got his courage up and began to think he might be able to get published himself. How could a colored elevator operator go about getting a book of poems published? Well, not everyone could have done it, but Paul was his mama's son.

He took some of the poems he'd written — mostly formal poems, but a few in dialect, too — and marched down to Dayton's United Brethren Publishing House. Lucky for him, William Blocher, the manager, was impressed enough by Paul's deacon bearing to take time to read the poems. He was impressed, but he was also a businessman, and it wasn't his job to lose money. So he made Paul an offer: the company would publish the poems if Paul would pay the printing costs. He said a run of five hundred copies would only cost Paul one hundred twenty-five dollars.

One hundred twenty-five dollars! He might as well have said a thousand. Paul was making four dollars a week running the elevator (and giving most of it to Matilda). He turned to go. But before he had taken five steps, Mr. Blocher had a change of heart. Could be he saw how downcast Paul was and felt sorry. Could be he decided the poems he'd read were just too good not to be published. One way or another, he offered to pay the printing costs himself and said that Paul could pay him back out of the earnings. When Paul accepted Mr. Blocher's offer, both men were taking a chance. People don't usually fall over each other trying to buy poetry books. What if Paul couldn't sell enough copies to repay Mr. Blocher?

Well, like I said, Lady Luck was smiling. *Oak and Ivy,* Paul's first book, came out in early December 1892, just in time for Christmas. When Central High's school newspaper ran an advertisement for the book, many of the teachers and students came to Paul to buy copies. Word spread, and Paul began to get orders from the Western Association of Writers and from fellow Callahan Building employees. In just two weeks he sold 125 copies of his first book, enough to pay Mr. Blocher the money he owed.

Paul's dedication for *Oak and Ivy* reads, "To her who has ever been my guide, teacher, and inspiration, My Mother, this little volume is affectionately inscribed." You'll remember how Matilda Dunbar had always hoped Paul would become a preacher. Well, I'm thinking that the first time she held *Oak and Ivy* in her hands and read those words, she knew that Paul was not going to be a preacher. No, sir.

A poet, that's what her son was. Matilda could be proud of that, but like as not, she might've been a little worried too. She probably knew what any writer will tell you: getting a book published is all well and good, but it's going to take more than one book to put food on the table.

Still, for now Paul was doing well. You want to remember that in those days even white folks had to make their own entertainment. They couldn't just switch on a radio or a TV—they had to seek out live performances. So almost right away, Paul found he could earn some extra money by giving poetry readings. He had a deep, musical voice, and he didn't have any trouble finding plenty of folks who were willing to pay for the pleasure of listening to him read his poetry at a church or club meeting.

The Poet and His Song

A song is but a little thing
And yet what joy it is to sing.
In hours of toil it gives me zest,
And when at eve I long for rest;
When cows come home along the bars,
    And in the fold I hear the bell,
As Night, the shepherd, herds his stars,
    I sing my song and all is well.

There are no ears to hear my lays,
No lips to lift a word of praise;
But still with faith unfaltering,

I live and laugh and love and sing.
What matters yon unheeding throng?
    They cannot feel my spirit's spell,
Since life is sweet and love is long,
    I sing my song and all is well.

My days are never days of ease,
I till my ground and prune my trees.
When ripened gold is all the plain,
I put my sickle to the grain.
I labor hard and toil and sweat,
    While others dream within the dell;
But even while my brow is wet,
    I sing my song and all is well.

Sometimes the sun, unkindly hot,
My garden makes a desert spot.
Sometimes a blight upon the tree
Takes all my fruit away from me;
And then with throes of bitter pain
    Rebellious passions rise and swell;
But—life is more than fruit or grain,
    And so I sing, and all is well.

One day in 1893, the editor of the *Herald* invited Paul to his office. Only two years earlier, that same editor had told Paul that Negroes couldn't work in the paper's editorial room. Can't you picture how puzzled — maybe even how wary — Paul must have been as he went through that office door?

He needn't have worried. Seeing how popular Paul's poems were getting, the editor had decided that even though Paul couldn't sit at a desk alongside whites, nothing said the young writer couldn't send in articles from afar. How would Paul like to go to Chicago and send back some stories from the World's Columbian Exposition, the first World's Fair ever held? Well, jump back. Paul wasn't about to cut off his nose to spite his face. He took the job.

You can bet that he didn't mind saying a sort of temporary good-bye to his elevator in the Callahan Building.

Paul hadn't been in Chicago but a bit when he met Frederick Douglass. Like Paul's parents, Douglass had been born a slave. During his early years, he had taught himself to read and write, and then, like Paul's daddy, he had managed to escape to the North. Afterwards, in the years before the Civil War, he became famous as a tireless and powerful orator. Speaking from his own experience, Douglass made the evils of slavery vivid and unforgettable to whites. In his writings and speeches, he promised blacks that learning to read, then forbidden to slaves, was the key that would unlock all other freedoms.

By the time Paul met Douglass, the orator was an old man but as tireless as ever. Paul was mighty tickled when Douglass offered him a job at the Haitian Pavilion as a kind of receptionist and personal secretary. All sorts of important people came to meet and exchange ideas with the famous orator. Paul got to meet them all.

I'll bet he had to pinch himself sometimes to believe it all was really happening, that he wasn't back in that Dayton elevator just having a daydream.

But think of it! Just twenty-one years old, and he really was there in the company of Frederick Douglass. The great orator's powerful presence impressed Paul so deeply that even in the poems of his late years, you can hear echoes of Douglass's convictions.

from The Unsung Heroes

A song for the unsung heroes who rose in the
    country's need,
When the life of the land was threatened by the
    slaver's cruel greed,
For the men who came from the cornfield, who came
    from the plough and the flail,
Who rallied round when they heard the sound of the
    mighty man of the rail.

They laid them down in the valleys, they laid them
    down in the wood,
And the world looked on at the work they did, and
    whispered, "It is good."
They fought their way on the hillside, they fought
    their way in the glen,
And God looked down on their sinews brown, and
    said, "I have made them men."

They went to the blue lines gladly, and the blue lines
      took them in,
And the men who saw their muskets' fire thought not
      of their dusky skin.
The gray lines rose and melted beneath their
      scathing showers,
And they said, "'T is true, they have force to do, these
      old slave boys of ours."
. . . .

Oh, Mighty God of the Battles Who held them in Thy
      hand,
Who gave them strength through the whole day's
      length, to fight for their native land,
They are lying dead on the hillsides, they are lying
      dead on the plain,
And we have not fire to smite the lyre and sing them
      one brief strain.

Give, Thou, some seer the power to sing them in their
      might,
The men who feared the master's whip, but did not
      fear the fight;
That he may tell of their virtues as minstrels did of
      old,
Till the pride of face and the hate of race grow
      obsolete and cold.

How do you suppose Paul felt when the fair was over
and he went back to his elevator in Dayton? I reckon he felt
that no matter what floor he was going to, every trip was a

"down." Up there in Chicago, thanks to Frederick Douglass, he hadn't been just one of the thousands wandering around the Exposition. He'd had a place where he belonged, where he could talk freely, as an equal, with famous and intelligent men and women.

But back home? People didn't get on the elevator in the Callahan Building expecting to carry on a conversation with a colored man. They wouldn't think to ask the "elevator boy" about anything, 'cept maybe the weather. Paul had come home from Chicago with ideas just bursting to be shared — but who could he share them with?

Sometimes I think Paul must have felt like he was two different people. He was Paul Dunbar, a "colored" from Dayton, Ohio, who grew up listening to the inventive, musical dialect most all his neighbors and relatives spoke and who was sometimes addressed as "boy" (or worse) by whites who didn't know anything about him and could see no further than the color of his skin. And he was Paul Laurence Dunbar, who wrote poems, plays, and novels in the standard English he learned from his mother at home, who was admired and praised by important people both black and white — people who invited him into their homes and flocked to his readings and lectures.

But I don't want you to think that I'm making this out to be simple or clear-cut. Living with one foot planted in one world and the other foot planted in another is a balancing act. Not easy. It's not like one day Paul put on his Paul Dunbar hat and wrote a dialect poem that hearkened back to his upbringing and then the next day he changed to his Paul *Laurence* Dunbar hat and composed a formal poem revealing an educated man of extraordinary poetic genius.

It seems to me if you look closely at his poetry, you'll find a little bit of each Paul in most any of his poems. Maybe the two Pauls weren't really so different after all. Take a look at these two poems now, one in dialect, the second in standard English:

An Ante-Bellum Sermon

We is gathahed hyeah, my brothahs,
    In dis howlin' wildaness,
Fer to speak some words of comfo't
    To each othah in distress.
An' we chooses fer ouah subjic'
    Dis — we'll 'splain it by an' by;
"An' de Lawd said Moses, Moses,
    An' de man said, 'Hyeah am I.'"

Now ole Pher'oh, down in Egypt,
    Was de wuss man evah bo'n,
An' he had de Hebrew chillun,
    Down dah wukin' in his co'n;
'Twell de Lawd got tiahed o' his foolin'
    An' sez he: "I'll let him know —
Look hyeah, Moses, go tell Pher'oh
    Fu' to let dem chillun go.

An' ef he refuse do it,
    I will make him rue de houah,
Fu' I'll empty down on Egypt
    All de vials of my powah."

Yes, he did—an' Pher'oh's ahmy
    Wasn't wuth a ha'f a dime;
Fu' de Lawd will he'p his chillun'
    You kin trust him ev'ry time.

An' yo' enemies may 'sail you
    In de back an' in de front;
But de Lawd is all aroun' you,
    Fu' to ba' de battle's brunt.
Dey kin fo'ge yo'chains an' shackles
    F'om de mountains to de sea;
But de Lawd will sen' some Moses
    Fu' to set his chillun free.

An' de lan' shall hyeah his thundah,
    Lak a blas' f'om Gab'el's ho'n,
Fu' de Lawd of hosts is mighty
    When he girds his ahmor on.
But fu' feah some one mistakes me,
    I will pause right hyeah to say,
Dat I'm still a-preachin' ancient,
    I ain't talkin' 'bout to-day.

But I tell you, fellah christuns,
    Things 'll happen mighty strange;
Now, de Lawd done dis fu' Isrul,
    An' his ways don't nevah change,
An' de love he showed to Isrul
    Wasn't all on Isrul spent;
Now don't run an' tell yo' mastahs
    Dat I's preachin' discontent.

'Cause I isn't; I'se a-judgin'
    Bible people by deir ac's;
I'se a-givin' you de Scriptuah,
    I'se a-handin' you de fac's.
Cose ole Pher'oh believed in slav'ry,
    But de Lawd he let him see,
Dat de people he put bref in, —
    Evah mothah's son was free.

An' dah's othahs thinks lak Pher'oh,
    But dey calls de Scriptuah liar,
Fu' de Bible says "a servant
    Is a worthy of his hire."
An' you cain't git roun' nor thoo dat,
    An' you cain't git ovah it,
Fu' whatevah place you git in,
    Dis hyeah Bible too 'll fit.

So you see de Lawd's intention,
    Evah sence de worl' began,
Was dat His almighty freedom
    Should belong to evah man,
But I think it would be bettah,
    Ef I'd pause agin to say,
Dat I'm talkin' 'bout ouah freedom
    In a Bibleistic way.

But de Moses is a-comin',
    An' he's comin', suah and fas'
We kin hyeah his feet a-trompin',
    We kin hyeah his trumpit blas'.

But I want to wa'n you people,
    Don't you git too brigity;
An' don't you git to braggin'
    'Bout dese things, you wait an' see.

But when Moses wif his powah
    Comes an' sets us chillun free,
We will praise de gracious Mastah
    Dat has gin us liberty;
An' we'll shout ouah halleluyahs,
    On dat mighty reck'nin' day,
When we'se reco'nized ez citiz'—
    Huh uh! Chillun, let us pray!

And now for the second:

We Wear the Mask

We wear the mask that grins and lies,
It hides our cheeks and shades our eyes—
This debt we pay to human guile;
With torn and bleeding hearts we smile
And mouth with myriad subtleties,

Why should the world be over-wise.
In counting all our tears and sighs?
Nay, let them only see us, while
We wear the mask.

We smile, but oh great Christ, our cries
To Thee from tortured souls arise.
We sing, but oh the clay is vile
Beneath our feet, and long the mile,
But let the world dream otherwise,
We wear the mask!

In the first poem, we're hearing a preacher sermonizing to a group of slaves. (Anytime I read it, I can almost see him giving a little wink now and then. He's being careful what he says, but he's making sure his listeners catch his whole meaning.) Then, when you read the second poem, don't you wonder who the "We" is? Is Paul talking about folks like the preacher? All black people? Or is he talking about himself?

Two very different styles, but to my mind, in both poems, Paul's talking about the same thing. That's just my opinion, now. Studying a poem isn't like solving a problem in math. In math, two plus two makes four, right? But in a poem, two plus two may make five or six—just depends on how deep you dig.

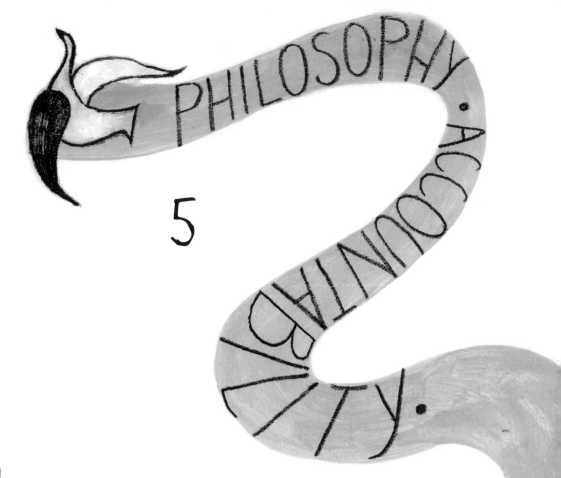

PHILOSOPHY · ACCOUNTABILITY ·

5

Chicago was behind Paul, but his need for more money wasn't. With his earnings from *Oak and Ivy*, he had made a down payment on a house for Matilda. He'd been feeling flush then, and optimistic, and maybe he forgot that after down payments, no matter how easy they are, come monthly payments. They come a lot more regular than poem sales do, and they have to be paid.

Still, poem sales help, so Paul kept on writing. He didn't just write, he traveled — farther and farther — for his speaking engagements. He spoke in Indiana, in Kentucky, in Michigan. And he spoke in Toledo, Ohio, which turned out to be one of the luckiest speeches he ever gave.

Now, if you've learned your Ohio geography, you know that Dayton and Toledo are about as far from each other as you can get and still be in the state. Dayton's near the bottom of the state, and Toledo's way up at the top, right next to Lake Erie. Are you wondering how it happened that Paul gave a speech up there?

Well now, to explain that, I'll have to go back a little. After *Oak and Ivy* came out, Paul began getting all sorts of letters praising his poetry. And of course he read them all. I reckon getting those first letters about his poems must have been one of the most exciting things that had happened to him so far. (And I can guess how Matilda's mama-pride swelled up every time the mailman delivered another handful of envelopes personally addressed to Mr. Paul Laurence Dunbar.) One of the letters came from Toledo, from a lawyer by the name of Charles Thatcher. I don't know was it Paul or Matilda brought in the mail that day, but I'm guessing that when they read *Charles A. Thatcher, Attorney at Law,* on the envelope, they made sure the letter got opened mighty quick. Unexpected letters from attorneys aren't letters you ignore. They don't always tell you something you want to hear.

But this one did. Turns out Mr. Thatcher had read some of Paul's poetry and liked it a lot. His letter was full of compliments, so Paul wrote back to thank him. When Mr. Thatcher found out that Paul was going to speak in some churches in Detroit, Michigan, he suggested maybe Paul could stop in Toledo on his way up, so as the two of them could meet. (Are you noticing, child, that people seemed to write a lot more letters in those days?)

Well, Paul did stop, and Charles Thatcher was so impressed with Paul that he invited him to stop in again on the way home from Detroit to read his poems at a recital Mr. Thatcher would arrange. I guess Paul must have been in tip-top form the day he gave that recital, because after he was back home, he received another letter from Mr. Thatcher.

This time, the attorney wrote that he and a group of his friends were willing to lend Paul enough money to go to college.

I don't know just why it was, but Paul turned down the offer. Instead of being put off by Paul's response, Charles Thatcher began to look around for other ways to help. And while he was looking, Paul was back in Dayton, doing his best to make ends meet — to make the house payments and put food on the table.

For the next year, somehow the money never seemed to come in as fast as it went out. Paul and his mother did the best they could. They took in boarders, people who paid to stay in a room and get their meals in the Dunbar house. He kept his elevator job and took on any additional jobs he could get. One after another, the jobs failed to help enough, till it must have seemed to Paul that he was never going to get ahead. One time, even, he had to swallow his pride and ask Charles Thatcher for enough money to make his house payment that month. There's nothing like worrying about money to pull a man's spirits down.

Philosophy

I been t'inkin' 'bout de preachah; whut he said de
     othah night,
'Bout hit bein' people's dooty, fu' to keep dey faces
     bright;
How one ought to live so pleasant dat ouah tempah
     never riles,
Meetin' evahbody roun' us wid ouah very nicest smiles.

Dat 's all right, I ain't a-sputin' not a t'ing dat soun's
   lak fac',
But you don't ketch folks a-grinnin' wid a misery in de
   back;
An' you don't fin' dem a-smilin' w'en dey 's hongry ez
   kin be,
Leastways, dat 's how human natur' allus seems to
   'pear to me.

We is mos' all putty likely fu' to have our little cares,
An' I think we 'se doin' fus' rate w'en we jes' go long
   and bears,
Widout breakin' up ouah faces in a sickly so't o' grin,
W'en we knows dat in ouah innards we is p'intly mad
   ez sin.

Oh dey 's times fu' bein' pleasant an' fu' goin' smilin'
   roun',
'Cause I don't believe in people allus totin' roun' a
   frown,
But it 's easy 'nough to titter w'en de stew is smokin' hot,
But hit 's mighty ha'd to giggle w'en dey 's nuffin' in de
   pot.

It was time for another book—maybe a second one
would sell well enough for Paul to get a little ahead. But
where was he going to get the money to publish a second
book?

Maybe Lady Luck decided it was time to pay Paul
another visit or maybe Charles Thatcher had been busy

talking about Paul to his friends and other important people back up in Toledo, but howsoever it came about, H. A. Tobey, a psychiatrist who was the superintendent of the state hospital in Toledo, wrote to Paul praising his poems and ordering more copies of *Oak and Ivy.* Dr. Tobey wanted Paul to give a performance of his poems to the patients at the hospital. So Paul was off to Toledo again, where he met this man who would become his lifelong friend and benefactor. And the first happy result of the meeting was that in July of 1895, Thatcher and Tobey together offered to pay all the costs of printing a second book of Paul's poetry. Jump back!

Seems to me that when he started putting together his second book, Paul must have been listening to his heart and his head both. He'd been reading and studying poetry for years now, long enough to realize that his poems were just as good as some of those he'd studied in school. The poems written in the "proper English" Matilda admired, in traditional forms like sonnets and such, were poems Paul was willing to stake his reputation on. His only problem with them was deciding which ones to include. And for sure that's the kind of problem a poet doesn't mind working on.

Now I'm going to ask you a question. How many of your friends do you suppose would rather read serious poetry than any other kind of writing? More than adventure stories, or mysteries, or a good series?

Folks in Paul's time were a lot like folks today, and Paul wasn't anybody's fool. He knew that if he wanted this second book to sell, the poems in it had to be the kind most folks would want to read. He'd found that the *Oak and Ivy* poems using dialect were the ones people always wanted to talk about, and he probably suspected that some of his other dialect poems, with their storytelling and humor, would help make his new book popular. So he added a second section to the book he was planning, a smaller section, called "Humor and Dialect."

He named the new book *Majors and Minors,* to show the way he thought about the poems. Lots of folks have wondered over the years why he thought this way. As far as I know, he never said, and when you read the "minor" poems carefully, you can see that he must have worked as hard on them as he did on the others. All the things that make a poem sing — the rhymes, the rhythm, the pleasing sounds — the minors don't take a second place to the majors when it comes to those things. So I'm guessing he didn't think they were inferior in that way — technically, you might say.

But look at what poetry really is, the way Paul must have looked at it. Poems that sound like somebody talking? Poems about possums and "co'n pone" and "shadder" pictures? Poems that are funny? He admired James Whitcomb Riley, he wouldn't deny it, but none of the poets in his schoolbooks, the poets he hoped to be compared to, had written about things like these. In his experience, major poems were serious looks at *major* themes or subjects — like nature, or love, or war or death. The poems he thought of as minor (not all of which were in dialect) were on lighter themes, on topics from everyday life, and a lot of them were humorous.

Accountability

Folks aint got no right to censuah uthah folks about
    dey habits;

Him dat giv de squirls de bushtails made de bobtails
      fu' de rabbits.
Him dat built de grea' big mountains hollered out
      de little valleys,
Him dat made de streets an' driveways wasn't shamed
      to make de alleys.

We is all constructed diff'rent, d'ain't no two of us de
      same;
We can't he'p ouah likes an' dislikes, ef we'se bad we
      ain't to blame.
Ef we'se good, we needn't show off, case you bet it
      ain't ouah doin'
We gits into su'ttain channels dat we jes
      cain't he'p pu'suin'.

But we all fits into places dat no othah ones cud fill
An' we does the things we has to, big er little, good
      er ill.
John cain't tek de place o' Henry, Su an' Sally ain't
      alike;
Bass ain't nuthin' like a suckah, chub ain't nuthin' like
      a pike.

When you come to think about it, how it's all planned
      out it's splendid.
Nuthin's done er evah happens, 'dout hit's somefin'
      dat's intended;
Don't keer whut you does, you has to, an' hit sholy
      beats de dickens,—
Viney go put on de kittle, I got one o' mastah's chickens.

Majors and Minors wasn't so different from *Oak and Ivy,* but what happened after it came out was a lot different. William Dean Howells, a famous writer, reviewed the book in *Harper's Weekly,* a magazine just as famous as he was. Mr. Howells heaped praise on Paul and his poems. He especially liked the poems in dialect. Listen to what he had to say: "It is when we come to Mr. Dunbar's Minors that we feel ourselves in the presence of a man with a direct and fresh authority to do the kind of thing he is doing."

The *Harper's Weekly* article came out in June of 1896. People all over the States — people on farms, in small towns, in big cities — pulled the magazine from their mailboxes and read. You know how it is nowadays when a new band begins to catch on? Yesterday, you never heard of them; today everyone's talking about them, everyone wants to listen to their songs. That's pretty much what happened. People took their poetry seriously then, and right away, everyone wanted to read the poems of the young Negro poet Paul Laurence Dunbar.

Paul and his mother, having no idea of the effect the article was having, were on a short trip out of town. While they were gone, their poor mailman found himself with a big problem — more than two hundred letters had arrived for Paul, and there was no one in the house to give them to. Well, he figured it out. I always laugh when I think about this — Paul and Matilda going up their front walk, not believing their eyes. The mailman's solution had been to stuff all those letters behind the shutters on the front of the house. Think about how all those envelopes peeking out from behind the shutters must have looked! Too bad there wasn't someone there to take a picture.

When Paul opened the letters and found order after order for one, two, maybe three copies of *Majors and Minors,* it was his first hint of how Howells's article would affect his future. People had read the review, they had read the book, and sure enough, they loved his poetry, especially the dialect poems. Invitations urging Paul to come read his poems poured in from all over the country.

From then on, what with one thing and then another, Paul found himself doing the same kind of thing James Whitcomb Riley did: writing and performing poems he considered minor — poems in dialect.

The Poet

He sang of life, serenely sweet,
    With, now and then, a deeper note.
    From some high peak, nigh yet remote,
He voiced the world's absorbing beat.

He sang of love when earth was young,
    And Love, itself, was in his lays.
    But ah, the world, it turned to praise
A jingle in a broken tongue.

6

INVITATION TO LOVE

I suppose by now I've given you the notion that Paul just spent all his time at home writing poems. He was writing, all right, but besides new poems, he was writing letters that would change his life. Even before *Majors and Minors* came out, a poem and a picture in a magazine had caught his eye. The beautiful young girl in the picture was Alice Moore, a schoolteacher in New Orleans, and the poem was one of hers. Paul was smitten. He sat down and wrote a letter to her, in care of the magazine. After a time she answered, and they began exchanging letters. As the months went by, Paul's letters turned into a kind of courting, and Alice's letters back showed she was thinking that Alice Moore Dunbar might be a fine name for a girl.

Alice, now — there was a girl who was used to getting her own way. The story goes that when she told her mama, Patsy Moore, about Paul, Mrs. Moore was not impressed. Not one bit. She'd worked hard to get "up" in New Orleans society, and she was counting on this daughter of hers to make a "good" marriage. Light-skinned Alice was talented and beautiful. Paul was a poet with very black skin and an uncertain financial future. His mother had been a laundress, for goodness' sake! (I shouldn't be making fun, but that's the kind of person Alice's mama was.)

Knowing how her mother felt, Alice let on that the letters she and Paul were exchanging were not much more than friendly discussions of poetry and literature. Since Alice and Paul had never actually met face-to-face, and everyone knew that Alice was flirting with several eager and eligible young men, Patsy Moore wasn't suspicious. But seeing that Alice was Alice, she should have been. And if she had taken a good look at *Majors and Minors,* she would have seen in the "majors" a poem or two that might've raised her suspicions. One was titled simply "Alice," and close to it was this one below. If I'd been Patsy Moore, I might have judged it was high time to have a little talk with my daughter. Though, now that I think on it, and on what I know about Alice, I expect it would've taken more than a little talk to change Alice's mind about anything.

Invitation to Love

Come when the nights are bright with stars,
    Or come when the moon is mellow;
Come when the Sun his golden bars
    Drops on the hay-field yellow.
Come in the twilight soft and gray,
Come in the night or come in the day,

Come, oh Love, whene'er you may,
    And you are welcome, welcome.

You are sweet, oh love, dear Love,
You are soft as the nesting dove,
Come to my heart and bring it rest
As the bird flies home to its welcome nest.

Come when my heart is full of grief,
    Or when my heart is merry;
Come with the falling of the leaf,
    Or with the redd'ning cherry.
Come when the year's first blossom blows,
Come when the summer gleams and glows,
Come with the winter's drifting snows,
    And you are welcome, welcome.

Majors and Minors was published in 1896. Paul wasn't but twenty-four years old, Alice was in love with him, and folks all over the country were getting to know his name. They were reading his poems and buying his books. When he gave a performance, flocks of people came to see the handsome young poet with a voice like a musical instrument, the young man who could make you laugh and cry and sit up proud, he was that impressive. Were he and Matilda riding high? I'll say they were!

But while things were getting better for Paul, many things were getting worse for black people as a whole. Ever since the Emancipation Proclamation, people in both the North and the South had been trying to figure out how life would be now that black people weren't slaves anymore.

Seems like once the slaves were free, some people wanted to make sure they weren't *too* free. It was one thing to say black people shouldn't be slaves, but then to say it was okay for them to do anything a white could do? That was something else. That's how some people thought, and it was going to take more than a civil war to make them change their minds.

So those whites who thought that blacks should "know their place" set about showing the former slaves just what that place should be — where they could live, where they could work, who they could marry, and where their children could go to school. More and more Jim Crow laws — laws that set out what blacks could or (mostly) couldn't do — were passed and later repealed, and then maybe passed again with a few different words and a different name. Different places had different laws. After a while, there were so many of these Jim Crow laws a black person could hardly keep track. If you were black, the safest thing to do was stay away from the white part of town.

In 1896, the year that *Majors and Minors* came out, the Supreme Court of the United States decided that schools didn't have to let black children in as long as there was a "separate but equal" school nearby. Many schools like Paul's high school, that both black and white students could attend, were replaced by schools just for white children and separate schools that were supposed to be as good, but mostly weren't, for black children. The decision by the Court was called *Plessy v. Ferguson,* and it changed more than schools. From then on, because of the way the Court's decision was interpreted and applied, whites could keep blacks out of all sorts of places as long as there were "separate but equal" opportunities nearby. The effect of *Plessy* was to make blacks secondary citizens, and some whites made sure the blacks knew it.

Paul could see what was happening, little by little, insult by insult. He could write all the poems he wanted to, but the same white people who read and admired his poems and bought his books didn't seem to notice or care that there weren't any blacks in the hotels they stayed in, the public restrooms they used, or the train cars they rode in.

He probably wondered if this is what his dad had fought for. He might have brooded over these words of Frederick Douglass, spoken shortly after the Emancipation Proclamation:

> In a composite nation like ours as before the law, there should be no rich, no poor, no high, no low, no white, no black, but common country, common citizenship, equal rights and a common destiny.

And these, much later:

> Where justice is denied, where poverty is enforced, where ignorance prevails, and where any one class is made to feel that society is an organized conspiracy to oppress, rob, and degrade them, neither persons nor property would be safe.

In this next poem, seems to me you can almost hear an echo of the famous orator as Paul writes out his own anger and disillusion.

from **To the South**

On Its New Slavery

What, was it all for naught, those awful years
That drenched a groaning land with blood and tears?
Was it to leave this sly convenient hell,
That brother fighting his own brother fell?

When that great struggle held the world in awe,
And all the nations blanched at what they saw,
Did Sanctioned Slavery bow its conquered head
That this unsanctioned crime might rise instead?

Is it for this we all have felt the flame,—
This newer bondage and this deeper shame?
Nay, not for this, a nation's heroes bled,
And North and South with tears beheld their dead.

Whatever its intended and unintended effects, *Plessy v. Ferguson* was an example of how people attempted to sort out their differences legally. But not everyone was willing to let the law take its course. Secret, lawless groups across the South and in parts of the North kept terror alive with sudden, unpredictable threats and murders. The early Ku Klux Klan might have been rooted out, but its seeds of hate still sprouted up here and there.

It was about this time that Paul wrote the poem that follows. It's based on a true story, told to Paul by an old slave he met while he was living in Washington, D.C., and the man who was lynched was the old man's uncle. The poem was published by *Century Magazine* in 1900, but without its last two stanzas. I'm guessing the *Century* editor was afraid those eight eerie lines (about how the ghost of the dead man still haunts the men who murdered him) might be disturbing to some readers, so he just left them off!

The Haunted Oak

Pray why are you so bare, so bare,
　　Oh, bough of the old oak-tree;
And why, when I go through the shade you throw,
　　Runs a shudder over me?

My leaves were green as the best, I trow,
　　And sap ran free in my veins,
But I saw in the moonlight dim and weird
　　A guiltless victim's pains.

I bent me down to hear his sigh;
　　I shook with his gurgling moan,
And I trembled sore when they rode away,
　　And left him here alone.

They 'd charged him with the old, old crime,
　　And set him fast in jail:
Oh, why does the dog howl all night long,
　　And why does the night wind wail?

He prayed his prayer and he swore his oath,
    And he raised his hand to the sky;
But the beat of hoofs smote on his ear,
    And the steady tread drew nigh.

Who is it rides by night, by night,
    Over the moonlit road?
And what is the spur that keeps the pace,
    What is the galling goad?

And now they beat at the prison door,
    "Ho, keeper, do not stay!
We are friends of him whom you hold within,
    And we fain would take him away

"From those who ride fast on our heels
    With mind to do him wrong;
They have no care for his innocence,
    And the rope they bear is long."

They have fooled the jailer with lying words,
    They have fooled the man with lies;
The bolts unbar, the locks are drawn,
    And the great door open flies.

Now they have taken him from the jail,
    And hard and fast they ride,
And the leader laughs low down in his throat,
    As they halt my trunk beside.

Oh, the judge, he wore a mask of black,
　　And the doctor one of white,
And the minister, with his oldest son,
　　Was curiously bedight.

Oh, foolish man, why weep you now?
　　'T is but a little space,
And the time will come when these shall dread
　　The mem'ry of your face.

I feel the rope against my bark,
　　And the weight of him in my grain,
I feel in the throe of his final woe
　　The touch of my own last pain.

And never more shall leaves come forth
　　On a bough that bears the ban;
I am burned with dread, I am dried and dead,
　　From the curse of a guiltless man.

And ever the judge rides by, rides by,
　　And goes to hunt the deer,
And ever another rides his soul
　　In the guise of a mortal fear.

And ever the man he rides me hard,
　　And never a night stays he;
For I feel his curse as a haunted bough,
　　On the trunk of a haunted tree.

Did you notice it was in 1900 the poem appeared? Four years after *Plessy v. Ferguson*, thirty-five years after the Civil War ended, and still an editor was so afraid of how readers might react to Paul's poem that he wouldn't publish the whole thing! Now, Paul wasn't nobody's fool; he knew as well as the editor what the times were like. He wrote the poem anyway. And not just this one — other poems, too, as well as articles, short stories, and novels showing how things were. Sometimes he did it with a smile, and sometimes he did it with a sigh, but when he saw the need for his voice, he didn't let caution silence him.

No matter, there are always some folks who think the only way to get anywhere is by shouting, and over the years, there have been those who, although they weren't around at the time, claim Paul didn't do sufficient shouting.

In 1900 it didn't take much for the hooded men to decide you needed to learn a lesson. White or black, speak out against injustice too strongly and you could watch your house burn down some night. I don't recall ever seeing the word *brave* written alongside Paul's name, but if you ask me, "The Haunted Oak" might as well be a shout, and it took a brave man to voice it.

7

KISS THE BROW OF ALICE?

THE GARRET

There, now, I guess I strayed away from my story a little bit, didn't I? But I wanted you to see how things were in the years after *Majors and Minors* took Paul from being a Dayton poet to being an American poet.

All those letters, all those requests for visits and speeches—I'm thinking Paul might have found it all over-whelming. However it came about, Charles Thatcher and Dr. Tobey took it upon themselves to find someone who could take care of the business side of Paul's career. The man they approached was Major James B. Pond, who was also the agent for Mark Twain. (Now, I know you know the name Mark Twain—*Tom Sawyer* and all that? Jump back, Paul!) Major Pond agreed to take Paul on, so Dr. Tobey suggested that Paul should meet Major Pond in New York.

New York? That big city? Of course, it wasn't as big

then as it is now, but it was a whole lot bigger than Dayton. And Paul was supposed to go off there by himself to meet a man he didn't even know. Think about it — Paul surely must have. In New York, he could meet other writers, and Alice was now living in Boston, so he'd be a bit closer to her. Matilda was up in Chicago with Rob. Best of all, Major James B. Pond was promising he could help Paul publish more books and get more speaking engagements. It all sounded good, so Paul packed up and left.

For a while, Major Pond was as good as his word. He took Paul around the city and introduced him to publishers. When Dodd, Mead and Company agreed to publish *Lyrics of Lowly Life* with a good advance payment to its author, Paul's trust in Major Pond's judgment became complete. And when the Major said a reading tour in England was bound to be a big success, Paul was willing.

Now, you remember I told you Alice Moore was a young lady who liked to get her own way? When Paul wrote that he was leaving for England and would be gone some months, Alice decided he wasn't going to leave before the two of them had even met. It must have taken some doing, but she managed to slip away from Boston in time to go to a big good-bye party for Paul. The party, given by a friend of Alice's, was on the night before he left. How do you suppose Paul felt when the hostess whispered to him, "Alice is here," and he and Alice stood face-to-face at last? Jump back? I guess so. By the time the night was over, Alice and Paul were secretly engaged.

I expect I know what you're thinking, child. You're thinking, "How romantic!" And I suppose it was. But

remember, now. Paul had fallen in love with a picture and
a poem. Alice had fallen in love with a man who wrote love
poems especially for her, a poet whose fame she was expecting to share. It's true they'd been sending letters back and
forth for two years, but there's lots of things you need to
know about a person you plan to marry that you can't find
out in a letter. I know I'm spoiling the romance for you, so
I won't say any more now. They were young, and they were
in love, and no one could have told them a thing, if anyone'd
been there to tell them.

Alice

Know you winds that blow your course
    Down the verdant valleys,
That somewhere you must, perforce,
    Kiss the brow of Alice?
When her gentle face you find,
Kiss it softly, naughty wind.

Roses waving fair and sweet
    Thro' the garden alleys,
Grow into a glory meet
    For the eye of Alice;
Let the wind your offering bear
Of sweet perfume, faint and rare.

Lily holding crystal dew
    In your pure white chalice,
Nature kind hath fashioned you
    Like the soul of Alice;
It of purest white is wrought,
Filled with gems of crystal thought.

The next day Paul was off for England. What do you suppose he was thinking of when he stepped on board the ship that would take him across the ocean? Major Pond had promised that Paul would be speaking to groups of cultured, admiring listeners. Some of them might even have titles, like Sir Richard So-and-So or Lady Sarah, Duchess of Such-and-Such. What would people like that think of his poetry, particularly the dialect poems? He knew *Majors and Minors* had sold many copies in England, but . . .

If that was what he was worrying about, he was gnawing the wrong bone. Around then many English people had never seen a dark-skinned person, so they were curious about them. It's a lot easier to be around people who are curious about you than around people who've been taught that you're naturally lazy and dishonest, like many white folks in the States had been. And in England, Paul was not just a dark-skinned person; he was also a famous poet. He traveled all around England, giving performances everywhere. In letters back home to Matilda, he boasted that he was being treated with a kind of respect he'd never received before. No need to search for a "colored" drinking fountain, no hotels or restaurants with signs that said *Whites Only.* There must have been a jaunty spring in his step during those first months.

But there's never been a life that didn't have its ups and downs. Back in New York, Paul hadn't objected when he found out that it was the Major's daughter, not Major Pond himself, who would be making all the arrangements in England. His first thought might have been that if she was as good a promoter as her father, he would be in good hands. It probably wouldn't have been a bad idea to have a second thought then, but as far as I know, nobody's able to see into the future, so you can't really blame Paul for the way things turned out.

While Paul was in London, Miss Pond did manage to get Paul a very good advance for a British edition of *Lyrics of Lowly Life.* (Couldn't have been hard, with everyone clamoring to see Paul and hear him recite their favorite poem.)

But that was about the only helpful thing she did. And then she decided that she had more interesting things to do than look after Paul's interests. First she took off for France for a while, and then she went back to the United States.

Paul was left alone in England, with no one organizing further performances, no money coming in, and not much in the way of savings. He could have given up and gone home then and there, but he was Matilda's son, and he had learned from her how to make the best of things, so he rented an attic flat and began to work on his first novel.

Those last few months in England, now — surprisingly enough, I'm thinking they were some of the best months of Paul's whole life. With some small savings to live on, and no day-to-day responsibilities to anyone else, he could spend as much time as he wanted writing, and when he left his flat to wander around London, he didn't have to worry about running into trouble simply because his skin was black. But winter was coming on, and you don't want to face a London winter if you don't have warm winter clothes with you, and Paul didn't. He had to swallow his pride and write to Dr. Tobey. But even though he hadn't grown rich in England, he could still head home with more than he'd come with — the manuscript of his first novel, *The Uncalled.*

The Garret

Within a London garret high,
    Above the roofs and near the sky,
My ill-rewarding pen I ply
    To win me bread.
This little chamber, six by four,
Is castle, study, den, and more,—
Altho' no carpet decks the floor,
    Nor down, the bed.

My room is rather bleak and bare;
I only have one broken chair,
But then, there's plenty of fresh air,—
    Some light, beside.
What tho' I cannot ask my friends
To share with me my odds and ends,
A liberty my aerie lends,
    To most denied.

The bore who falters at the stair
No more shall be my curse and care,
And duns shall fail to find my lair
    With beastly bills.
When debts have grown and funds are short,
I find it rather pleasant sport
To live "above the common sort"
    With all their ills.

I write my rhymes and sing away,
And dawn may come or dusk or day:

Tho' fare be poor, my heart is gay,
      And full of glee.
Though chimney-pots be all my views;
'T is nearer for the winging Muse,
So I am sure she 'll not refuse
      To visit me.

When Paul came back from England in August 1897, newspapers wanted to interview him, invitations to speak were pouring in from all over, and he got a good-paying job as a clerk in the Library of Congress. Best of all, although no one but Matilda knew (he couldn't keep a secret from her), he was engaged.

The next March, he and Alice Moore were married. She resigned from her teaching job, and they moved into a house in Washington, D.C. That year Paul had a book of short stories and his first novel published. Then he and an old friend, Will Marion Cook, who was also a talented composer, collaborated on a musical, *Clorindy, or the Origin of the Cakewalk.* Right away it was a hit on Broadway. Paul wasn't but twenty-six years old, and he was already more famous than even Matilda could have expected him to be.

For the next few years, you couldn't stop Paul. He published more books of poetry and three more novels. He collaborated with Will Cook on two new musical plays. He was on top of the world professionally. Think, though — if you're on top, there's no place to go but down, is there?

Seems to me that Lady Luck left Paul's side the day that he and Alice were married. Like I said, his writing

wasn't a problem; it was going as well as anyone could ask. Paul's professional life wasn't giving him grief. But his personal life — don't say I didn't warn you. Like they say, even matches made in heaven have to be lived here on earth, and as much as they might have loved each other, neither Paul nor Alice exactly qualified for sainthood.

Almost at the very beginning of the marriage, Alice realized that dealing with Paul was going to be a sight harder than managing her mother had been. Alice had ambitions for Paul, and she had ideas about how a famous poet should behave. She also had opinions about Paul's writing — she was proud and happy when one of his poems in standard English was published, but she found the dialect poems embarrassing.

Paul's everyday speech was polished and courtly. He never spoke in dialect at home, so Alice couldn't understand why he kept writing dialect poems. They might have been helpful early, in winning Paul readers, but as far as Alice was concerned, now that his reputation was established, all the dialect poems did was remind people of his blackness.

Alice — beautiful, accomplished, light-skinned Alice — was used to passing as white when she chose to do so. Her family, especially her mama, were eager to rise in society. The particulars of their family background were things they'd just as soon not talk about.

On the other hand, during Paul's high-school years, when he was the only black student in his class, he was liked and accepted by classmates like the Wright brothers, and was even elected president of the school's prestigious debating club, the Philomena Society. Those years, along with his months in England, had given Paul a realistic acceptance of his (very) black skin. He wasn't ashamed of his skin color, and even if he had been, there was nothing he could do about it.

But to be fair to Alice, her question — when Paul could write standard-English poems that equaled those of any of his white peers, why did he choose to write and publish poems in dialect as well? — is one that all sorts of people have asked for years. It's like a hot potato that gets tossed around whenever Paul's name comes up. I'm going to give you some of my thoughts now, but really, no one but Paul knows the answer, and we can't ask him.

In the first place, like Paul realized early on, readers loved the dialect poems. They read them, they memorized them, they talked about them, and then they wanted more. More dialect poems brought more compliments, more sales, and consequently more money. Paul liked all three, and with a wife and a mother to support, how could he disappoint his readers? Why should he want to?

In the second place, Paul had an ear for dialect like nobody else. Once he said, "There are as many variations of the negro dialect as there are states in the Union! For instance an Alabama negro does not speak any more like a Virginia colored man than a Yankee talks like a man from Colorado." He knew, Paul did, that some white writers at that time were writing stories with Negro characters who were mostly just figures of fun, like the fools in plays by Shakespeare. These writers figured Negro dialect was just a bunch of grammar mistakes and made-up or mispronounced words. Hmph! Maybe Paul decided that if people wanted dialect in what they read, he could at least show them what authentic dialect was.

Just one more thing. The way I see it, Paul admired the family and the neighborhood he'd grown up with. Joshua, Matilda, Bud Burns — they and the old blacks whose stories of slavery and everyday life in the rural South he had listened to — I figure he wanted to share their stories, and he wanted to share their way of telling those stories too.

8

Now, like I said, Paul's professional life was going well, but his job at the Library of Congress, moving around dusty old books, aggravated his lungs until, on the very last day of 1898, he resigned. He figured he could support himself, his mother, and Alice solely through his writing if he exchanged those hours in the library for hours at his desk. (And so you know, child, from Paul's time to ours, not many poets have been able to manage something like that. It wasn't what I'd call an unrealistic plan, but it was ambitious. And it involved more than just sitting at a desk and scribbling lines on a piece of paper.)

Paul wrote and wrote. More poetry, of course, but more plays, too, more short stories, articles, and novels. Invitations to read his poetry kept coming from all over, and Paul accepted them whenever he could, because they usually paid well. So he traveled here, there, and everywhere. These trips were hard on him physically, and his frequent separations from Alice were hard on their marriage.

Traveling back then wasn't any cakewalk. You didn't just jump in your car or hop on an airplane and get where you wanted to go, quick as you needed to. Matter of fact, even walking or riding a streetcar to the train station was a job. Paul probably was lugging a suitcase, and I never saw a writer going anywhere that he wasn't carrying a book or two as well. Then, to get where he was going, he had to travel through a world that didn't give much thought to the needs of a black traveler. A long, uncomfortable journey in the only train car allotted to blacks (no matter if they were famous poets or not), a train car that was either too hot or too cold, depending on the time of year, and then a search for a public restroom, or a place to eat that didn't have a *Whites Only* sign above the door — it's no wonder Paul might have come home exhausted and surly.

Things being the way they were, I'm guessing that neither Paul nor Alice thought it was particularly worrisome that much of the time, Paul just didn't feel good. He kept going along like a man who is sure he'll feel better the next day. But the next day would come, and he wouldn't feel better. Not the next day nor the next nor the next. Then finally the day came when a doctor told Paul why he hadn't been getting better, and why he probably wouldn't in the future.

Remember I mentioned Paul's weak chest when he was young? Well, in those years, there was more tuberculosis around than there is now, and when the TB germ found Paul's chest, it settled in to stay. Joshua had died of TB, and so had Susan Wright, mother of Wilbur and Orville. How did Paul catch the germ? Whose cough sent it flying out into the same air he was breathing in? It might have been a friend, maybe someone in the front row at one of his readings, or a fellow passenger on a train. We'll never know, and what difference does it make? It happened, and that was that.

There was no cure for TB back then. If you got it, you were supposed to rest a lot. But Paul couldn't rest, or at least he thought he couldn't. Hardheaded is what I'd call him. He cut back on his speaking engagements, but he didn't turn them all down, not by a long shot. He did agree to trips with Alice to the Catskill Mountains, and then to Colorado, for the sake of his health.

But as for writing — why, writing was what he did. He couldn't stop doing that. Instead of resting, he would take a little whiskey to ease the pain. Those days, doctors often recommended that. Paul had always liked alcohol, maybe a little too much, and gradually a little became a lot, and like it does, too much drinking brought trouble. It was bad enough when he drank too much at home, but when he sometimes stumbled or stuttered at his readings, Alice was angry and embarrassed.

Paul and Alice began to argue more. Joshua Dunbar hadn't set an example of a good husband, and Paul — as much as he loved Alice — was not a good husband, either. (And Alice herself wasn't exactly an angel, I guess, because who is? But I'm telling you about Paul — Alice's story is for another day.)

Finally, in a temper one day in early 1902, Paul packed a suitcase and left. Alice had had enough. She locked him out of the house, and though he begged and pleaded, though he sent her letters and poems, she never saw or spoke to him again.

A Song

Thou art the soul of a summer's day,
Thou art the breath of the rose.
　　But the summer is fled
　　And the rose is dead
Where are they gone, who knows, who knows?

Thou art the blood of my heart o' hearts,
Thou art my soul's repose,
　　But my heart grows numb
　　And my soul is dumb
Where art thou, love, who knows, who knows?

Thou art the hope of my after years —
Sun for my winter snows
　　But the years go by
　　'Neath a clouded sky.
Where shall we meet, who knows, who knows?

Paul was heartbroken. He was sick and getting sicker. He stayed on in Washington for a while, and then he decided to go back to Dayton. Maybe if he spent some time resting there, his health would improve. Matilda could care for him, and his old friend Bud could do some smart doctoring. But even back home, Paul couldn't seem to rest. He listened when Matilda and Bud told him he needed to take it easy, but then he went right ahead and accepted another speaking engagement that would take him out of town again. He wrote and gave readings as often and as long as he could, and in 1905 he got an invitation he couldn't refuse. I'm not sure anyone could have. President Theodore Roosevelt invited Paul to ride in his inaugural parade. An invitation like that for someone who once was just another colored boy from Dayton's West End? Of course he was going. Jump back, honey!

Back in Dayton, after the excitement of the triumphant Washington parade, Paul knew he was getting worse. He rested more often and let his mother care for him. He spent most of each day up in his bedroom. When he was well enough to talk to visitors, he was as good-humored and charming as ever. Sometimes, on good days, he would talk Matilda into letting him visit with friends on the front porch, where his border collie puppy gave visitors a rambunctious welcome. Another pet he had was a young black chicken that liked to fly up and snuggle down on his shoulder.

More and more often, though, Paul had to turn to Bud for help. But not even Bud could work miracles. Not for Paul and not for himself. Unexpectedly, late in 1905, Bud died.

It was Bud whom Alice had tasked with warning her if Paul should grow worse. She wanted to see her husband one more time before he died, and she was counting on Bud to let her know if she needed to make a quick trip to Dayton. But a few months later, when Paul took his final turn for the worse, no one knew to inform Alice.

Paul Laurence Dunbar, America's most beloved black poet, died on February 9, 1906, at the age of thirty-three. His mother was by his side. His wife found out about his death by reading a notice in the newspaper.

Matilda Dunbar lived on in the house Paul had bought

for her. For the next twenty-eight years, she kept his room just the way he had left it. She wouldn't even let folks sleep in his bedroom — anyone staying the night, they had to go up to the attic to sleep.

Two years after Matilda died, the Ohio Historical Society bought the house. Paul's room was still just as he'd left it. To this day, if you go on a tour of the Dunbar House, you will see his toothbrush still sitting in a glass in the bathroom.

A Death Song

Lay me down beneaf de willers in de grass,
Whah de branchs 'll go a-singin' as it pass.
    An' w'en I's a-layin' low,
    I kin hyeah it as it go
Singin', "Sleep, my honey, tek yo' res' at las'."

Lay me nigh to whah hit meks a little pool,
An' de watah stan's so quiet lak an' cool,
    Whah de little birds in spring,
    Ust to come an' drink an' sing,
An' de chillen waded on dey way to school.

Let me settle w'en my shouldahs draps dey load
Nigh enough to hyeah de noises in de road;
    Fu' I t'ink de las' long res'
    Gwine to soothe my sperrit bes'
Ef I's layin' 'mong de t'ings I's allus knowed.

Now before you get all upset with me for giving you a sad ending, child, just remember this. Paul's writing didn't die when he did. For years after his death, folks would recite "Little Brown Baby," "A Negro Love Song," "When Malindy Sings," and other poems that they loved and memorized.

And "Sympathy"? Today, if you just say the line, "I know why the caged bird sings," right away folks will nod and smile, even if they don't recognize the poem's title. You don't have to be black to understand the longing in that poem, to feel its sadness.

I'm guessing both Paul and Matilda would be proud that today "We Wear the Mask" and "Sympathy" are such famous poems. And I'm hoping they might be even happier to learn that the dialect poems aren't dismissed as "jingles in a broken tongue," but are valued as accurate renderings of the rich and varied black language and culture Paul knew so well.

Paul wasn't always happy, but then most people aren't always happy. Maybe that's why folks keep coming back to his poetry. It's because they know where it comes from — they've been there, too. So I think it's only right to let him have the last word, don't you?

Bein' Back Home

Home agin, an' home to stay—
Yes, it's nice to be away.
Plenty things to do an' see,
But the old place seems to me
Jest about the proper thing.
Mebbe 'ts 'cause the mem'ries cling
Closer 'round yore place o' birth
'N ary other spot on earth.

W'y it's nice jest settin' here,
Lookin' out an' seein' clear,
'Thout no smoke, ner dust, ner haze
In these sweet October days.
What's as good as that there lane,
Kind o' browned from last night's rain?
'Pears like home has got the start
When the goal's a feller's heart.

What's as good as that there jay
Screechin' up'ards towards the gray
Skies? An' tell me, what's as fine
As that full–leafed pumpkin vine?
Tow'rin' buildin's—yes, they're good;
But in sight o' field and wood,
Then a feller understan's
'Bout the house not made with han's.

Let the others rant an' roam
When they git away from home;
Jest gi' me my old settee
An' my pipe beneath a tree;
Sight o' medders green an' still,
Now and then a gentle hill,
Apple orchards, full o' fruit,
Nigh a cider press to boot—

That's the thing jest done up brown;
D'want to be too nigh to town;
Want to have the smells an' sights,
An' the dreams o' long still nights,
With the friends you used to know
In the keerless long ago—
Same old cronies, same old folks,
Same old cider, same old jokes.

Say, it's nice a–gittin' back,
When yore pulse is growin' slack,
An' yore breath begins to wheeze
Like a fair–set valley breeze;
Kind o' nice to set aroun'
On the old familiar groun',
Knowin' that when Death does come,
That he'll find you right at home.

AUTHOR'S NOTE

For years, I wanted to write a book about Paul Laurence Dunbar, the famous poet from Dayton, Ohio. I, too, was born in Dayton, although Dunbar had died a good many years before. Some people who had known him or heard him perform were still alive then, but I don't remember that I ever met any of them. I wish I had—think what they might have been able to tell me!

The first step in writing a biography is to gather information. Learning all I could about Dunbar, his family, his career, and his times was fun for me. I read book after book, article after article. I studied, I took notes—I did everything but write. I was scared.

Up to then, my books had all been fiction—most of them written for very young boys and girls. Writing a biography, especially a biography for young readers, is a tremendous responsibility. Unless you know your subject personally and have a chance to talk with him or her, most of the information you can get comes from others—and these others may not agree with one another. What do you do then? Which information should you accept, and which should you reject? Or do you try to include everything? I fretted; I stewed; I read more books. I did everything but write that first sentence. Time went by, and I began to think that perhaps I should drop the idea and stick to picture books.

Then, one day, sitting at my computer, staring at the still-empty screen, I heard a voice say, "You never heard of Paul Laurence Dunbar? Child, where've you been? I got to have a word with you." Whose voice was it? I had no idea. It was a grandma voice for sure, but not my grandma's. I thought it might belong to my lost friend Emma. Emma was a grandma who was younger than I, but she considered herself wiser in many ways. (She was right.) As a matter of fact, I knew several grandmas from our church in the Northside area of Cincinnati with the same combination of colorful speech and decisive opinions. Was it one of them I heard?

It wasn't long until I decided it didn't matter. Whoever had spoken those words had something to say. And once I'd heard her voice, I knew how to write the story.

So while I was writing *Jump Back, Paul,* I let Grandma do the telling. Like all grandmas she had her own ideas — about Paul, about Alice, about Paul's poetry, about how the story should go. I could be fretting about a missing piece of information and she would say, "Why's that important? You can nose it out after a while, if you think you have to. Let's just get on with the telling for now." Sometimes we argued. I'd say, "I don't know what to write here. Some experts think one thing and some think another." And she'd answer impatiently, "Those people wrote their own books. This one's yours. You need to write what *you* think."

So that's what I did. With Grandma's help.

CHRONOLOGY

January 1, 1863   President Lincoln signs the Emancipation Proclamation.

April 9, 1865   The Civil War ends with General Robert E. Lee surrendering to General Ulysses S. Grant at Appomattox Court House, Virginia.

June 27, 1872   Paul Laurence Dunbar is born in Dayton, Ohio.

March 26, 1874   Paul's sister, Elizabeth (Liza) Florence Dunbar is born.

January 9, 1876   Matilda Dunbar files for divorce from Joshua Dunbar.

May 30, 1876   Liza Dunbar dies.

August 16, 1885   Joshua Dunbar dies.

Fall 1886   Paul enters Central High School.

June–July 1888   The Dayton *Herald* publishes "Our Martyred Soldiers" and "On the River."

June 16, 1891   Paul graduates from Central High School.

1891   Paul takes a job as an elevator operator in the Callahan Building in Dayton.

June 27, 1892   On his twentieth birthday, Paul presents a poem of welcome to the Western Association of Writers convention at Dayton's Grand Opera House.

July 26, 1892   The *Indianapolis Journal* prints James Newton Matthews' letter praising Paul and his poetry.

November 27, 1892   James Whitcomb Riley sends Paul an encouraging letter.

1892   William A. Blocher of United Brethren Printing Company advances money to pay printing costs of *Oak and Ivy*.

May–October 1893 Paul goes to Chicago to report on events at the World's First Columbian Exposition. He becomes a personal assistant to Frederick Douglass.

1894 Paul meets Charles A. Thatcher of Toledo, Ohio, and Dr. H. A. Tobey, superintendent of Toledo State Hospital.

April 17, 1895 Paul writes to Alice Ruth Moore after reading one of her poems and seeing her picture in the *Boston Monthly Review*.

May 18, 1896 In *Plessy v. Ferguson,* the Supreme Court establishes the "separate but equal" clause.

1896 *Majors and Minors* is released, published by Hadley and Hadley of Toledo, with publishing costs covered by Thatcher and Tobey.

June 27, 1896 William Dean Howells' review of *Majors and Minors* is published in *Harper's Weekly*.

1896 Major James Pond becomes Dunbar's agent and arranges for publication of *Lyrics of Lowly Life.*

February 5, 1897 The night before Paul leaves for England, he and Alice meet and become engaged.

August 1897 Paul returns from England.

October 1897 Paul begins to work at the Library of Congress.

March 6, 1898 Paul and Alice marry secretly.

December 31, 1898 Paul resigns his position at the Library of Congress.

1898–1902 Prolific years of writing and speaking, but Paul's health declines and his and Alice's marital problems increase.

May 1899 Paul collapses, told his lungs are in bad shape.

January 25, 1902 Paul leaves Alice.

December 17, 1903   Orville Wright makes one of the first powered heavier-than-air airplane flights at Kitty Hawk, North Carolina.

1903   Paul and his mother move back to Dayton.

March 4, 1905   Paul takes part in Theodore Roosevelt's inaugural parade.

November 19, 1905   Bud Burns dies unexpectedly.

February 9, 1906   Paul Laurence Dunbar dies.

February 24, 1934   Matilda Dunbar dies.

Source Notes and Side Trips on the Research Journey

Chapter 1

Joshua Dunbar

Because Paul's father, Joshua Dunbar, died when Paul was only thirteen, by the time anyone began to think about writing Paul's biography, facts about Joshua were hard to come by. Even Paul's most careful biographers differ on some important points. So if you decide to read up on Joshua, bear in mind who's doing the telling, even if it's Paul or Matilda, the two who should know the most. Remember what Granny always says: "There's more than one way to tell the truth." A good place to begin, though, is "Joshua Dunbar's Family Tree," at the Dayton Aviation Heritage National Historical Park website, listed in the bibliography.

The U.S. Colored Troops

At the beginning of the Civil War, many African Americans, including former slaves, wanted to fight for the Union, but a 1792 federal law had effectively excluded Negroes from the U.S. Army. However, that didn't stop some officers from accepting black volunteers or setting up groups of black troops, and finally, on May 22, 1863, the government issued General Order 143, which created the United States Colored Troops. The first authorized black regiments were from South Carolina, Tennessee, and Massachusetts.

"General Order 143," Our documents: 100 Milestone Documents from the National Archives, http://www.ourdocuments.gov/doc.php?doc=35.

Matilda Burton Murphy Dunbar

Paul's mother was born into slavery in Kentucky around 1845. Before the Civil War, when she was only about sixteen, her owner married her to a slave from a different plantation, R. W. Murphy. They had a son together, but during the war, Murphy went off to fight and never came back. Matilda was pregnant with their second son, so as soon as the Emancipation Proclamation freed her, she took the older boy and moved to Dayton, Ohio, where her mother and grandmother were living. There she met Joshua Dunbar. They married on December 24, 1871. To my way of thinking, Matilda was a remarkable woman. Someday someone should write her biography, and "Matilda Burton Murphy Dunbar's Family Tree," at the Dayton Aviation Heritage National Historical Park website, listed in the bibliography, is a good place to start finding out more of her story.

Paul's Siblings

Paul's older half brother, William Travis (Buddy) Murphy, was born in Kentucky, on February 12, 1864, so, like his parents, he was born into slavery. He was only two when he and Matilda, who was expecting another child, moved to Dayton to live with Matilda's mother. We know Buddy finished ninth grade, later married, and settled in Chicago, but in later years Paul and Matilda saw a lot more of Paul's other half brother, Rob, than they did of Buddy. He died in Chicago, in 1932, two years before Matilda.

Robert Small Murphy, or Rob, as he was called, was the younger of Paul's two half brothers. Like Paul, he was born free, on August 1, 1866, at the home of Matilda's mother on Howard Street in Dayton. Not quite six when Paul was born, Rob followed Buddy's path throughout his younger years. He left school after the eighth grade and went to work as a janitor at the Beckel House, the same Dayton hotel where Buddy worked. After his own marriage, Rob followed Buddy to Chicago, where he became an employee of the Chicago public schools. Both Matilda and Paul lived with Rob and his family now and then over the years, and the two brothers always stayed close. According to biographer Virginia Cunningham, the day before Paul died, he asked Matilda to send for Rob. Rob was present at Paul's funeral, and later at Matilda's. At the time of his death, sometime after 1940, he was the last of Paul's immediate family.

You don't hear much about Paul's little sister, Elizabeth Florence Dunbar, who lived only from March 1874 to May 1876. It seems she wasn't ever strong or healthy, and Paul's biographers don't agree about the cause of her death. Some sources attribute it to malnutrition, some cite kidney failure or other ailments. Matilda never stopped mourning her only daughter and late in life told an interviewer, "As a baby [she] was brighter than Paul. If only my little girl had lived."

Alexander, p. 32.
Cunningham, pp. 2–3.
Dayton Aviation Heritage National Historical Park website.

Dayton's Rivers

The Great Miami, the Stillwater, Mad River, and Wolf Creek all flow through or around Dayton on their way down to the Ohio. Paul and his friends had plenty of choices for either swimming and fishing, and many of his poems show how much he loved the rivers for their beauty, as well.

Chapter 2

Central High School

Central High School was a three-story square brick building on the corner of Fourth and Wilkinson Streets in Dayton. Paul was originally a member of the class of 1890 but graduated with the class of 1891 because he had to repeat a math class. Central High School was razed in 1893 and replaced by Steele High School, an imposing stone building on a corner of Main and Monument.

Various articles, Dayton History Books Online, http://www.daytonhistorybooks.com.

William Anderson (Bud) Burns

Bud Burns, who was a year younger than Paul, was one of the few African-American students at Central High School. He was the son of Anderson Burns and Mary Ella Finley, and after the death of his parents, he lived at the home of Captain Charles Stivers, the principal of Central High School, earning the money he needed for school by working as the Stiverses' yardman. After graduation, he attended medical school at Western Reserve University in Cleveland, Ohio. He returned to Dayton in 1898 and became the city's first African-American physician. Whenever Paul was in Dayton, Bud acted as his personal physician. He was a trustee of the Dayton Academy of Medicine in 1903 and 1904, as well as a captain and assistant surgeon in the Ohio National

Guard. He died unexpectedly, of typhoid fever, on November 19, 1905. According to *The Military Surgeon,* "At a special meeting of the Academy it was voted to attend the funeral in a body and resolutions setting forth the respect of the Academy for Dr. Burns and its regret at his untimely death were unanimously adopted."

Quite a success story for someone with a background like Bud's, wouldn't you say?

Cunningham, p. 333.

The Military Surgeon 20, no. 1 (January 1907).

William Burns entry, "Deaths," *Journal of the American Medical Association* 45 (December 2, 1905) p. 1750.

Herald Poems

The Dayton *Herald* printed "Our Martyred Soldiers" on June 8, 1888, and "On the River" on July 13, 1888.

Cunningham, p. 30.

Central High Graduation Song

Program, Class of 1891, Commencement Exercises of Central High School at Grand Opera House, June 16, 1891, MSS 659, series 1, box 1, Paul Laurence Dunbar Papers, Ohio Historical Society, Columbus.

Chapter 3

The Western Association of Writers

The Western Association of Writers was organized in 1886 to support and promote the literary works of authors in Midwestern states such as Indiana, Ohio, Illinois, and Missouri. Three famous members were Booth Tarkington; two-time winner of the Pulitzer Prize for Fiction; Lew Wallace, author of *Ben-Hur;* and James Whitcomb Riley, the "Hoosier Poet." The group met yearly for nineteen years (1886–1904).

Western Association of Writers, Collection Information, State of Indiana website, http://in.gov/library/fa_index/fa_by_letter/w/1217 html.

Dr. James Newton Matthews

When Paul met Dr. Matthews, the doctor already had an established reputation as a poet as well as a country doctor. Known as the "Poet of the Prairie," he had published multiple popular volumes of poetry, and he did all he could to encourage Paul and spread his reputation. Dr. Matthews' devotion to poetry did not take away from his commitment to his patients, and he died of a heart attack at the age of fifty-eight after trudging five miles through a snowstorm to treat a patient.

James N. Matthews Papers, 1868–1872, 1966–1968, record series number 41/20/26, University of Illinois Archives.

p. 34: "chained like a galley slave . . . starvation wages": quoted in Martin, p. 15.

Letter from James Whitcomb Riley

Riley's letter, dated November 27, 1892, is written on the stationary of Denver, Colorado's Brown Palace Hotel, underneath the hotel's slogan, "Absolutely Fireproof." Riley tells the young poet, "Certainly your gift — as evidenced by this 'Drowsy Day' poem alone — is a superior one." He closes the letter with the phrase "your friend" and signs his full name, James Whitcomb Riley, in elegant script.

James Whitcomb Riley to Paul Laurence Dunbar, November 27, 1892, MSS 114, series 1, box 1, Paul Laurence Dunbar Papers, Ohio Historical Society, Columbus.

"Little Orphant Annie"

On March 8, 1924 the front page of the *Indianapolis Star* featured the photograph and obituary of Mary Alice Smith Gray. She had been identified in 1915 as the original Little Orphant Annie, the ten-year-old hired girl who lived in Riley's childhood home, caring for the four children as well as doing the housework asked of her. On winter evenings, she would sit with the children by the fireplace and tell them stories of ghosts and goblins.

"Orphant Annie's Obituary," James Whitcomb Riley website, http://www .jameswhitcombriley.com/orphant_annie's_obituary.htm.

Chapter 4

William Lawrence Blocher

It would be a shame not to tell you a little bit about William Lawrence Blocher, whose change of heart had such a pivotal effect on Paul's life. Like Bud Burns, Blocher was left an orphan at a young age. He was only eleven when his father was killed on a

Civil War battlefield. For five years, he lived and worked on a local farm in exchange for room, board, and clothing. During the winter months, he was allowed time to attend school. He spent his teenage years learning the printing trade at the *Mercer* (Ohio) *County Standard,* then moved to Dayton and got a job at the United Brethren Publishing House, where he was made foreman of his department (with the ability to make department decisions) only a year before he met with Paul. Maybe Blocher's own impoverished background led him to take a chance on Paul, but I'm guessing that he had a knack for making good decisions, because by the time he retired, he was superintendent of the entire manufacturing department of the United Brethren Publishing House. Not bad for an orphan who started with nothing!

William Lawrence Blocher entry, "Centennial Portrait and Biographical Record of the City of Dayton and of Montgomery County, Ohio," Dayton History Books Online, http://www.daytonhistorybooks.com/page/page/1697325.htm.

The Haitian Pavilion

Because Frederick Douglass had been U.S. ambassador to Haiti, he was invited to represent that country at the Columbian Exposition. His courage in speaking his mind at the dedication of the pavilion must have made a deep impression on Paul. Douglass said: "Haiti is black, and we have not yet forgiven Haiti for being black or forgiven the Almighty for making her black. In this enlightened act of repentance and forgiveness, our boasted civilization is far behind all other nations. In every other country on the globe a citizen of Haiti is sure of civil treatment. In every other nation his manhood is recognized and respected. Wherever any man can go, he can go. He is not repulsed, excluded or insulted because of his color. All places of amusement and instruction are open to him. Vastly different is the case with him when he ventures within the border of the United States."

"Lecture on Haiti," January 2, 1893, Frederick Douglass Papers, Library of Congress, http://www.loc.gov/item/mfd000473.

Chapter 5

Dr. Henry A. Tobey

In the 1800s, the lightness or darkness of a Negro's skin was considered to be an indication of how much inherited "white" blood he had in him. Several biographers recount Dr. Tobey's exclamation to the friend who accompanied him to the train station for his first meeting with Paul, "Thank God he is Black!" In Toby Gentry's excellent biography of Paul he included Tobey's quick explanation, "I meant thank God he's dark enough so that whatever genius he may have cannot be attributed to white blood."

By all accounts, Dr. Tobey, who was remarkably free of the racial stereotypes many people in the 1800s entertained, became not only Paul's mentor but a steadfast, lifelong friend. Paul sometimes stayed at the Tobey home, where Dr. Tobey's three girls treated him like a member of the family.

Gentry, p. 54.

William Dean Howells' Review of *Majors and Minors*

William Dean Howells, "Review of Paul Laurence Dunbar, "Majors and
    Minors,'" *Harper's Weekly,* June 27, 1896: pp. 630–631.
Publishers' Bindings Online, http://binding.lib.ua.edu/gallery/dunbar_harpers.htm.

Chapter 6

Alice Ruth Moore Dunbar

When Alice's answering letter finally arrived, the first sentence explained the legitimate reason for her delay in answering, for she began, "Dear Sir: — Your letter was handed me at a singularly inopportune moment — the house was on fire." She then explains that "after the house was declared safe," she was still hampered by a burn on her hand and eyes irritated by smoke.

With Paul's death in 1906, Alice was left a young, childless widow. Living and teaching in Wilmington, Delaware, she published essays, poems, and newspaper and scholarly articles to augment her meager teacher's salary.

Although she married two more times, she kept Dunbar as part of her surname throughout her life. In later years, in addition to writing, she was active in political affairs, particularly those affecting women and African Americans. She died in Philadelphia at the age of sixty, in September 1935.

Alice Ruth Moore to Paul Laurence Dunbar, May 7, 1895, series 1, box 1, Paul Laurence Dunbar Papers, Ohio Historical Society, Columbus.

Jim Crow

Jim Crow was the name of a fictional slave, an object of ridicule, originated by a white performer, Thomas Dartmouth Rice, who performed throughout the 1830s and 40s. Made up in blackface and using a crude imitation of Negro dialect, Rice made his Jim Crow such a popular figure of fun that as soon as any white comedian blackened his face, the audience recognized him as Jim Crow. The name became so familiar that people began to attach it to any law or regulation or custom aimed at restricting African Americans.

"The Origins of Jim Crow," Jim Crow Museum of Racist Memorabilia, Ferris State University, http://www.ferris.edu/jimcrow/origins.htm.

Frederick Douglass Quotations

p. 71: "In a composite nation . . . common destiny": "Composite Nation," 1867, Frederick Douglass Papers, Library of Congress, http://www.loc.gov/item/mfd000405.

p. 71: "Where justice is denied . . . would be safe": excerpt from Frederick Douglass, "The Nation's Problem," 1889, Teaching American History website, http://www.teachingamericanhistory.org/library/document/the-nations-problem.

Century Magazine

Paul Laurence Dunbar, "The Haunted Oak," *Century Magazine* 61, no. 2 (December 1900): pp. 276–277.

Curiously, the essay that follows "The Haunted Oak" in the magazine is a thoroughly racist article entitled "Paths of Hope for the Negro: Practical Suggestions of a Southerner" by Jerome Dowd.

Chapter 7

Will Marion Cook

Will Marion Cook and Paul met through Frederick Douglass at the Haitian Pavilion during the Columbian Exposition. Cook's musical talent was apparent early, and at fifteen he was already studying violin at Oberlin College. In spite of his talent, he was unable to find employment at institutions of classical music, so he turned to popular music, writing songs inspired in part by the black folk music he had heard as a young boy staying with his grandfather in Chattanooga, Tennessee. He and Paul began collaborating on scores for musicals, and their first, *Clorindy, or the Origin of the Cakewalk,* was financially successful enough to be followed by others. From then on, Cook went from one success to another in a variety of musical venues. He influenced a generation of young black musicians, including Duke Ellington, who often referred to him as "Dad."

"Will Marion Cook (1869–1944) [biography]," Library of Congress Performing Arts Encyclopedia website, http://lcweb2.loc.gov/diglib/ihas/loc.natlib.ihas.200038839/default.html.
"The Ghost in Your iPod," John H. McWhorter, *City Journal,* http://www.city-journal.org/2008/18_4_urb=will_marion_cook.html.

The Cakewalk

Many articles and books are available to learn about the origin of the cakewalk. They all agree that it began as a slave walk or dance on southern plantations, winding up with the presentation of a cake to the most successful participants. Some say it was just for fun; some say it was a sly imitation of the dances of plantation owners. Whichever it was, its association with relaxation and fun resulted in the modern meaning of something that is easy and effortless.

Dunbar on Dialect

p. 89: "There are as many variations . . . from Colorado": quoted in Dunbar, *Life and Works,* p. 109.

SELECTED BIBLIOGRAPHY

BOOKS

Alexander, Eleanor. *Lyrics of Sunshine and Shadow: The Tragic Courtship and Marriage of Paul Laurence Dunbar and Alice Ruth Moore.* New York: New York University Press, 2001.

Best, Felton O. *Crossing the Color Line: A Biography of Paul Laurence Dunbar, 1872–1906.* Dubuque, IA: Kendall/Hunt, 1996.

Bryan, Ashley, ed. *I Greet the Dawn: Poems by Paul Laurence Dunbar.* New York: Atheneum, 1978.

Cunningham, Virginia. *Paul Laurence Dunbar and His Song.* New York: Dodd, Mead, 1969.

Davidson, Cathy N., and Linda Wagner-Martin, eds. *The Oxford Companion to Women's Writing in the United States.* New York: Oxford University Press, 1995.

Dunbar, Paul Laurence. *The Collected Poetry of Paul Laurence Dunbar.* Edited by Joanne M. Braxton. Charlottesville: University Press of Virginia, 1993.

———. *The Life and Works of Paul Laurence Dunbar: Containing His Complete Poetical Works, His Best Short Stories, Numerous Anecdotes and a Complete Biography of the Famous Poet.* Edited by Lida Keck Wiggins. Naperville, IL: J. L. Nichols, 1907.

———. *The Paul Laurence Dunbar Reader.* Edited by Jay Martin and Gossie H. Hudson. New York: Dodd, Mead, 1975.

———. *Selected Poems.* Edited by Herbert Woodward Martin. New York: Penguin, 2004.

Dunbar-Nelson, Alice Moore. *Give Us Each Day: The Diary of Alice Dunbar-Nelson.* Edited by Gloria T. Hull. New York: Norton, 1984.

Gentry, Tony. *Paul Laurence Dunbar.* New York: Chelsea House, 1989.

Gould, Jean. *That Dunbar Boy.* New York: Dodd, Mead, 1958.

Honious, Ann. *What Dreams We Have: The Wright Brothers and Their Hometown of Dayton, Ohio.* Fort Washington, PA: Eastern National, 2003.

Martin, Jay, ed. *A Singer in the Dawn: Reinterpretations of Paul Laurence Dunbar.* New York: Dodd, Mead, 1975.

McKissack, Patricia C. *Paul Laurence Dunbar: A Poet to Remember.* Chicago: Children's Press, 1984.

Page, Yolanda Williams, ed. *Icons of African American Literature: The Black Literary World.* Santa Barbara, CA: Greenwood, 2011.

Reef, Catherine. *Paul Laurence Dunbar: Portrait of a Poet.* Berkeley Heights, NJ: Enslow, 2000.

Revell, Peter. *Paul Laurence Dunbar.* Boston: Twane, 1979.

Riley, James Whitcomb. *Riley Child-Rhymes with Hoosier Pictures.* Indianapolis: Bowen-Merrill, 1899.

Schultz, Perle Henriksen. *Paul Laurence Dunbar: Black Poet Laureate.* Champaign, IL: Garrard, 1974.

Strickland, Michael R. *African-American Poets.* Springfield, NJ: Enslow, 1996.

Watson, Claudia. *Dayton Comes of Age: The City Through the Eyes of John H. Patterson, 1897–1922.* Dayton, OH: Montgomery County Historical Society, 2002.

WEBSITE

Dayton Aviation Heritage National Historical Park website. History and Culture, People, "Dunbar Family History." http://www.nps.gov/daav/historyculture /people.htm.

ACKNOWLEDGMENTS

It is always somewhat risky to write about someone whose culture is not your own. I am not of the same sex, race, or time period as Paul Laurence Dunbar. But almost seventy years ago, my fourth-grade teacher, Mrs. Patterson, read his "Little Brown Baby" aloud and told us that Dunbar had been born "right here in Dayton." Her words gave us an illogical sense of proud kinship with him that I never lost. Sadly, over the years, Dunbar's reputation has faded, until today even some Dayton schoolchildren are unfamiliar with his poetry. I hope that *Jump Back, Paul* will restore some of the recognition Dunbar deserves. I have the following people to thank for helping me to pursue that aim:

Dr. Herbert Woodward Martin, professor emeritus of the University of Dayton, poet and Dunbar scholar, who generously took the time to critique my text for accuracy and voice. Few people know and love Dunbar's work as much as Dr. Martin does, and few have done as much to preserve and promote Dunbar's legacy.

The legendary Ashley Bryan, artist, poet and lecturer, who graciously reviewed and responded to an early, unpolished draft of the manuscript.

Dr. Joanne M. Braxton, professor of humanities at the College of William and Mary, noted scholar, author, and lecturer, whose work, including her edition of *The Collected Poetry of Paul Laurence Dunbar,* has been influential in inspiring a growing appreciation of Dunbar's poetry.

I would have been at a loss researching Paul's story without the professional expertise of many librarians and archivists. Personnel at the Wright State Paul Laurence Dunbar Library in Dayton, Ohio; at the Paul Laurence Dunbar House, in Dayton, Ohio; and at the Ohio State History Center in Columbus, Ohio were all generous with their assistance. I owe particular recognition to Shawna Woodard, genealogy librarian at Dayton Metro Library for locating information on Dr. William (Bud) Burns; to Steven Greenberg at the National Library of Medicine for supplying information on the history of the American Medical Association; and to Helen F. Sullivan, MLS, at the University of Illinois for directing me to sources for Dr. James N. Matthews.

I am incredibly grateful to my editor, Andrea Tompa. Andrea is every writer's dream editor — attentive, accessible, and absolutely true to her word. To copyeditor Hannah Mahoney and proofreader Linda Arends go my heartfelt thanks for the many hours they spent meticulously reviewing these pages so that the book could be as factually accurate and error-free as possible.

Much of the enjoyment of reading a book comes through our physical senses; my sincere appreciation goes to book designer Amy Berniker for her expertise in choosing components that combined into a harmonious whole. Thank you, Amy, for a volume that is a joy both to see and to hold.

In this regard, I offer my utmost gratitude to Sean Qualls for his appreciative interpretation of Paul's poems and for the sensitivity of his tender illustrations.

In addition, I need to thank the members of my Cincinnati Writers' Group, Andrea Cheng, Cathryn Long, David Richardson, Mary Ann Rosswurm, Linda Leopold Strauss, Kathy Wiechman, and Connie Wooldridge, for giving me the courage to undertake my first foray into nonfiction and for providing support from first draft to last.

Among the many friends without whom I could not have persevered, I would like to thank especially author Sylvia Waugh of Great Britain. For over twenty years, our correspondence has sustained me, and I believe she has anticipated the release of this book as impatiently as I have.

Finally, thank you to my husband, Karl. No one has ever believed in me more. What an incredible gift.

INDEX